ON BEING GIFTED

ON BEING GIFTED

Written by the participants in the
National Student Symposium
on the Education of the Gifted and Talented

Mark L. Krueger, Project Director

Sponsored by The American Association For Gifted Children

Walker and Company
NEW YORK

Several indented quotations, the first of which appears on page 22, are reprinted by permission of Felice A. Kaufmann, Former Director, Project SPARKLE, Norwich, Connecticut, Public Schools.

This project was supported in part by the Robert Sterling Clark Foundation and a grant from the Office for Gifted and Talented, US Office of Education. Points of view or opinions, however, do not necessarily represent the official view or opinions of the Office of Education.

First published in the United States of America
in 1978 by the Walker Publishing Company, Inc.

Published simultaneously in Canada by Beaverbooks,
Limited, Pickering, Ontario.

Cloth ISBN: 0-8027-0616-9
Paper ISBN: 0-8027-7138-6

Library of Congress Catalog Card Number: 78-58622

Printed in the United States of America
10 9 8 7 6 5 4 3 2 1

371.95
K

YOU ARE HOLDING A UNIQUE BOOK

You are holding a unique book. For just as *The Double Helix* presented a new paradigm in reporting with astonishing candor the human process by which a major scientific discovery—DNA—was made, so, too, this small book in its own way offers a similarly inventive paradigm for bright, motivated students to communicate their experiences in gaining the initiative in learning. We hope that, unlike *The Double Helix* which remains curiously one-of-a-kind, *On Being Gifted* will spark further student initiatives in "seizing the tiller" (Teilhard de Chardin's phrase) of their education and development by working skillfully with parents, teachers, and other guides, and sharing the results.

The strength and beauty of the book come from the immediacy of personal experiences openly shared. Until now, our information about gifted youth came only from a few scholarly studies and occasional autobiographies by persons of high achievement. Biographies focus too seldom on the critical circumstances that coalesced a gift or talent; autobiographies are often written toward the end of an individual's life when youth is only half remembered. To date, no compendium of biographical data has been made to discover and compare the role that experiences of childhood and adolescence play in shaping the later contributions of gifted adults.

This book breaks fresh ground. It is not stuffy; it is almost free of the cant and jargon of the education field. It is the voice of 20 students who have worked together and achieved a harmony of purpose without losing their separate keys, chords, colors, and resonances. It is direct, candid, not satisfied, occasionally frustrated, sometimes witty, full of expectation.

It is the voice of a friend who doesn't have all the answers but who has walked this path a few steps ahead of you, the reader, another bright student, who is on the verge of taking charge of your own education. You can pick and choose what may be useful, argue with what nettles you, and then pass on your experience, perhaps with this book, to another. By doing so, the path for those who follow will be, if not less rigorous, at least more plainly marked.

Above all, we hope that this book gives you the courage to chase a dancing star.

SCOTT MCVAY

Contents

Preface

THIS book, essentially by and for gifted students, is also the result of close cooperation among many persons and organizations interested in these exceptional young people. Each contributed a vital component to this, the final product of the National Student Symposium on the Education of the Gifted and Talented, a project designed to focus constructively on the concerns of gifted students and to help them to consider ways of assuming more responsibility for their own education and development.

The idea for the entire enterprise originated with Scott McVay, then executive director of the Robert Sterling Clark Foundation in New York. He and his board of directors believed that the publication of a book of high quality, a truly imaginative piece of work, would be a valuable resource to any young person who wants to gain the initiative in both learning and life.

In an effort to augment the funds the Clark Foundation could commit, McVay consulted Harold C. Lyon, the director, and Jane Case Williams, the deputy director, of the Office for Gifted and Talented (OGT) of the U. S. Office of Education. This Office has assumed as one of its responsibilities the encouragement of programs co-sponsored by the public and private sectors aimed at strengthening the education of children and youth with exceptional potential. In this instance, OGT staff became the essential link between the public agencies and the private groups involved and provided needed office space and back-up services as well.

State departments of education, local school districts, and other agencies all assisted in identifying a pool of gifted young people from which twenty were eventually chosen to participate in the Symposium. These agency administrators first selected a pool of potential participants, all of whom had shown exceptional promise in a number of areas as well as interest in the project. The Symposium staff and advisors then made the final selection, one which attempted to insure that all the many different types of giftedness—academic, psycho-social, artistic, and creative—as well as varied personal backgrounds would be represented.

Necessary arrangements were made to provide for students' travel expenses to each of the meetings, the first in New York City, the next on the Eastern Shore of Maryland; the Clark Foundation grant provided funds to cover the expenses of the meetings themselves, consultants' fees, and other costs.

The American Association for Gifted Children served as administrative and fiscal agent and was actively involved in the organization and development of the program. Staff and members of the Association served as resource persons and, importantly too, gave a warm, supportive welcome to students upon their arrival in New York, many of whom were there for the first time.

The National/State Leadership Training Institute on the Gifted/Talented in Reston, Virginia, a federally funded project to encourage the development of gifted programs, provided additional financial support to cover costs incurred. In addition, the Institute's directors were most helpful in planning the Symposium.

Due to the interest of Everett Kinstler, the National Arts Club, a national historic landmark in New York, made space available for the first meeting of the Symposium. The Wye Institute, through the courtesy of James Nelson, its director, contributed its fine meeting and recreational facilities on the Eastern Shore of Maryland for the second session.

Reflecting their long interest in gifted children, the Council for Exceptional Children, located in the metropolitan Washington, D. C. area, contributed staff time for program planning and undertook with funds from the U. S. Office of Education, to provide reference copies of the book.

A full list of individual staff and consultants in the Symposium may be found in Appendix B. Of that staff, student authors had an eloquent spokesman for their concerns throughout the entire project in its director, Mark L. Krueger, a gifted young student then concurrently serving as an intern in the Office for Gifted and Talented. Uniquely fitted for his role, Krueger worked particularly well with the young people who participated in the Symposium.

By sharing their experiences of growing up gifted in an informal panel discussion at the first meeting, a group of gifted adults were tremendously supportive to the student participants. Chaired by Anne E. Impellizzeri, President of The American Association for Gifted Children, this panel included Jack Faxon, President Pro-Tempore, Senate of the State of Michigan; Amaziah Howell, Special Assistant to Senator James Buckley of the State of New York; Carl Sagan, Professor of Astrophysics, Cornell University; and Murry Sidlin, Resident Conductor, National Symphony Orchestra, all relatively young but already outstanding in their professions.

The efforts of the people and organizations mentioned above would have come to nought but for the gifted authors themselves. All are listed in Appendix A and all contributed their efforts, seriously, and steadfastly even in the midst of a thousand other demands. Their patience must be especially commended, for drafts and re-drafts of the manuscript flew back and forth across the country over many months.

Final editing of the manuscript is the work of Margery Thompson of Washington, D. C. Thompson was involved with the Symposium since its inception, working to see that the students' ideas always found their way onto paper. Hers is an exceptional job of editing, for it is faithful to the writing and ideas of the students themselves and in no way distorts what they expressed.

The concerns about educational opportunities found in this book apply not only to students like the participants but to all young Americans. Not every one of their thoughts is earthshattering; some of the educational experiences they describe can be found in many high schools around the nation. This is to be expected, for the students themselves do not claim to be authorities on anything but their own lives. Their thoughts, however, are all important because they are their own and not those of "experts." For this, the rest of us can only thank them for their hard work, their candor, and their willingness to provide that which we can only learn from the gifted—the joys and pains of being different.

MARJORIE L. CRAIG
Vice-President and Executive Director
The American Association
   for Gifted Children

Introduction

YOU are now reading a *book*, a real, complete printed book written and edited by twenty teenage students considered to be "gifted and talented" by the powers that be. We were asked to participate in what was called the National Student Symposium on the Education of the Gifted and Talented. The goal of this Symposium: to write and produce the first-*ever* (so far as we know) book *about* education of the gifted and talented—particularly on how to assume some responsibility for their own education. Tall order, right? It hasn't been easy, so maybe you will be interested in who we are and how we got from there to here.

Our first meeting took place in New York City on April 5-7, 1975 at the National Arts Club. All twenty of us were, at that time, 17 and 18 year old high school juniors or seniors, with one exception—a 15 year old sophomore at Johns Hopkins University. We are from various parts of the country, New Mexico to New York, North Carolina to Nebraska and, we have been told, well represent different types of giftedness. At least we soon learned that there was a considerable range of interests in the group sometimes all found within one person—music, art, science, poetry, foreign languages, and so on. And we each certainly had—and have—our own ideas about what is important to us.

To get to know one another and to generate as many ideas as possible was the first order of business in that New York meeting. The catalyst for our creative thoughts throughout most of the initial conference was Dr. Sidney J. Parnes, Professor of Creative Studies at the State University College of New York at Buffalo.

In a relaxed atmosphere, Parnes worked successfully to "speed up the creative process" given the time limits of the Symposium. The first day culminated with a division into four topical groups for brainstorming sessions from which came many ideas about any and all material we might want to cover. The next day, we met with a panel of four successful gifted adults in which panelists discussed their experiences, answered our questions, and later spoke with those of us who were interested. After that, we went over methods of gathering our material.

On our third and last day in New York, we got down to the actual format of the book. We decided that rather than tie ourselves to a concrete structure, we would leave most of the compilation and editing to our next conferences to be held about a month later at the Wye Institute in Queenstown, Maryland. In the meantime, participants would review various plans for assuming responsibilities related to their own education and development, if possible test some, and then write about these and previous experiences.

At our second meeting, the same group minus two members got down to work on the book itself. After reviewing the material which we had written over the five-week period, we decided to organize the book into nine chapters and parceled out the topics among the group. Then, students working in teams both compiled their assigned chapters and wrote sections for others as well. As we worked long tiring hours, five of our chapters merged into two, and eventually everything we wanted to include was covered.

One of us, a junior at Walbrook Senior High School in Baltimore, was chosen as editor, and we all left with three Xeroxed chapters in hand and more copies to follow. A lot of ideas were put on paper—some overlapping others—and many loose ends left dangling, and we knew that we still had many months to go and considerable editing to do before we were through. Still, we had completed the most vital aspect of the project—that of organizing the structure (such as it is) and the content.

Much of that original material has been rewritten and edited in view of everyone's comments. We have kept in touch with one another over these months and with the project director, who was our switchboard and our general contact with the Symposium's sponsors. Finally, in the fall of 1976, we were ready to turn over the manuscript to our professional editorial consultant for a final polish before publication.

Who is our audience? We're aiming in no uncertain terms at perhaps three million students who can be classified as "gifted and talented;" another aim is the teachers, parents of these students, as well as civic leaders and school officials. Our ultimate goal is to effect some change so as to provide better educational opportunities for the gifted and talented. We know, however, that while we can take responsibility for our education and development, we can't do it all or go at it alone.

It would help immeasurably if we knew exactly *who* these three million individual "targets" were, but we can't say precisely who is and who is not "gifted and talented." For years, people have tried to write definitions of the term (which can be offensive or prejudicial to some ears, as you may have noticed); none have completely succeeded. More about that later. For now, let's just say that we're writing the book for you who are gifted and talented or who have potential to be so; past that, we have no idea about finding you or knowing who you are. Since some of us are but were never told until lately that we were gifted, there must be some of you out there in the same state. So if you select yourself for the title, that's all right, too. *With us, it is the motivation that counts, not the name.*

About our own motivation, now, not to say our qualifications for writing this book: *The only advantage we have over others who have done comprehensive studies is the tremendous one, we think: we are living out the experience of being gifted.* While we may not be

Introduction

experts on education and probably have brought up ideas others have thought of and used before, we claim to be experts on being us. So, in the first part of the book, we have been very personal in relating experiences that seem to us to have some meaning for the rest of you who are gifted, too. Our last chapters are mainly about education, and we hope to offer more in the way of possible alternatives, should you need help in moving your own educational programs along. Some of our thoughts about both of these areas that we think are especially important appear in capital letters.

In each personal vignette, we haven't used names —not to protect the innocent—but mainly because we think it is the experience that is important, not the name. Where individuals differ will be very apparent. We are all listed in the back of the book, anyway—and we all take responsibility for the end result.

Chapter I

On Being Gifted

BEFORE launching into this whole subject, we're going to try to clear the air by offering a definition of "gifted and talented." We don't take credit for it, but we can say it is the definition that governs Federal programs —and by extension those of state and local agencies —for the "gifted and talented." We'd like to caution you that this definition is not universally accepted; to this day, no one has pinned down such nebulous terms as "gifted" or "ability"; presently, no one can accurately measure a person's creativity or skill. Bear with us; you can compare your personal concept of "gifted and talented" to ours a little later. But first, let's match ours with that of the professionals.

The following is taken from the 1971 *Report to the Congress on the Education of the Gifted and Talented* made by the U. S. Commissioner of Education:

Gifted and talented children are those identified by professionally qualified persons who by virtue of outstanding abilities are capable of high performance. These are children

1

who require differentiated educational programs and/or services beyond those normally provided by the regular school program in order to realize their contribution to self and society.

Children capable of high performance include those with demonstrated achievement and/or potential ability in any of the following areas, singly or in combination:

1. general intellectual ability
2. specific academic aptitude
3. creative or productive thinking
4. leadership ability
5. visual and performing arts
6. psychomotor ability

It can be assumed that utilization of these criteria for identification of the gifted and talented will encompass a minimum of 3 to 5 percent of the school population.

If you believe you possess such abilities, you might benefit from this book. Even if you're not sure you meet *any* definition to the letter, don't get upset and (for heaven's sake!) don't put us down. You may not fit into the Commissioner's definition, but that's not necessarily your seal of doom; it may just mean you will have to push a little harder on your own, which is what we hope we are about here.

What about our reactions to the Commissioner's report: *We* feel that to a certain extent giftedness is a way of thinking, a style of thought and an attitude which may include a super-motivation to learn or to do.

So far, not too much of a departure from the professionals. But we also feel that somewhere in their definition a point is being missed that we'd like to make, and it has to do with that phrase "identified by professionally qualified persons." To us, giftedness is a state of being; it *is*, whether or not it is identified by others. Some of us see the gifted as any person who feels disappointed with his education because it is not sufficiently challenging and who thinks that the fault lies with something external to himself. More precisely, we mean we troubled ones. While many gifted and many just bright students are satisfied with their educational position, they are not the targets of this book. Our ideas are perhaps every bit as unsatisfying as the Commissioner's and open the field to egotists, a number of religious fanatics, and all critics of the educational system. Perhaps all of our definitions used together are useful. Although this might class satisfied gifted kids as non-gifted, it would make a very nice operational definition for educators and the unrecognized gifted themselves.

What we are striving for right here is just something to give you an idea about whether you should go on to read the rest of the book, and we feel we have presented that. We are addressing this simply at *you*. Yes, we said *you*; pay attention next time!

"Talented" is not as easy to define, although it is the more commonplace word. In a manner of speaking, and in at least some areas, everyone is "talented," whereas it is generally conceded (and we agree) that not everyone can be called "gifted." The catch phrase is again "at a level greater than the norm." It may be argued that everyone is "talented" to some extent, but we're looking for something above and beyond the median. Aren't we always?

As you've probably noticed, we've had a little trouble in dealing with these terms—as who hasn't. So we'd like to present some of our individual views of giftedness. These plus the comments on being "gifted" threaded throughout this book—how we feel and how we react to being labeled as such—may in the end become a pretty fair definition in itself.

Gifted Is—Alienating

Probably the only single thing all twenty of us agreed on back in New York—and in our lives—was that we hate the word "gifted." It's flattering, it's pleasing, but it alienates us from friends. "Talented" we like; you can call us talented any time you like, folks.

Gifted Is—Creativity

Eleven years ago a school in North Carolina was set up by the state strictly for the performing arts. Recently a program in the visual arts, which I am majoring in, was added. Having referred to the terms "gifted and talented" before, I have come to the conclusion that most of the students at North Carolina School of the Arts are very talented or else they wouldn't be there; but when I refer to "gifted" I am referring to creativity and I feel creativity is a gift.

＿＿＿＿

Gifted Is—Natural Ability

My definition of the phrase "gifted and talented" would mean someone who is naturally able to do certain things, such as a student who has the ability to do schoolwork without much difficulty or someone who can succeed even in small things which only require a particular skill.

This phrase (like any other) is just a label. Every individual is quite unique with distinctive qualities about him—he only needs to manifest them. *I never considered myself to be gifted or talented, but I try hard to enhance my own natural abilities by bettering them.*

＿＿＿＿

Gifted Is—Choices

I'm one of those few people who try to do everything from serving as chairman of the parish bicentennial committee, to being a cheerleader, or a writer. I may not be very good in everything I do, but I do the best I can with only 24 hours in a day. I would list every little thing that I do, but if I saw it I don't think I'd believe it either!

Having multiple "talents" (I use the word loosely) allows you to dabble into a lot of different things. Consequently, you learn a little about a lot of things—which I think is important in order that you develop a broad spectrum of diverse interests, and in the process, meet hundreds of very interesting people. The best advantage from having these interests is that you seem to at least be able to find *some* parallel for comparison when with another person. Another aspect of having diverse interests is that it gives you a deep appreciation of life. You can never stop changing.

Gifted Is—Motivation?

Many of the most successful students in Independent Learning Experience, a program primarily aimed at gifted students which is described later in the book, would not be considered either gifted or talented in the sense of the Commissioner's report. They are, however, highly motivated. Why and in what sort of programs this occurs is a central question.

Okay, let's see what we have. The gifted and talented are a hazily defined group which must be dealt with on an individual basis. Fine. Yet, when other students are dealt with in this way, they also perform superbly. The answer seems clear. *Personal, humane, and stimulating education is what everyone needs. It seems to me that all children would be better off if they were treated in this way.*

Gifted Is—Responsibility to Self and Society

Being gifted, I have a strong sense of future, because people are always telling me how well I will do when I grow up. This humanistic kind of attitude begins to grow on you and one's sense of confidence swells in direct proportion with one's head. My feelings fluctuate from a sense of responsibility for everything to a kind of "leave me alone, quit pushing . . . " In general I think that I am in a good position, and I feel mostly an obligation to everyone and everything (even to myself) to "do well" in whatever sense I define it to be. I think that one must overcome the semiparanoid feeling that "people are jealous," that people hate you because you're gifted. Even if it is true, it is just an obstacle you should overcome, and I think you should regard it simply as such.

Gifted Is—Me?

I've never felt gifted. *It's really hard to write about*

being gifted since I never realized I was. School has always been easy. I've always been smarter than everyone else, but I never thought anything of it.

I've never been in any special programs. Until this year, I had never even heard of being gifted. I'm not advanced in my classes, although they're never challenging.

As for school, it has always been boring, but I never rebelled. I do talk a lot in class, but no one sees me as a discipline problem.

They tell me I'm gifted, so I suppose I am. Until now I didn't care. *Recently I've decided that if I'm so smart, maybe I should do something with my life.*

━━━━

In our definitions, we have singled out the troubled—and we have given more than a hint that being gifted is not all shredded wheat. Well, it is and it isn't. We've also said that the one thing we do know about giftedness is how it feels, how it affects your life, your relationship with others.

We know that scholars have tested, measured, researched, and described the characteristics of the gifted but descriptions are a far cry from living in that sensitive skin. We think that in studying people like us, the researchers—scholars though they may be—lose track of some of our human aspects, so we are writing about these things here.

In doing so, we draw on our own experiences, of course, but we have also included a few comments from

others to show that we are not alone in thinking the way
we do. You will find indented quotes scattered in these
pages from a group of third, fourth, and fifth graders in
a special gifted class in New England.* Their feelings
about the life and the label of "gifted" remind us of our
younger selves. And they don't even seem to mind the
label as much as we do. (Whenever the remarks come
from a different person, you will find the paragraph
separated by the following device ⚊⚊⚊.)

Now, let's be blunt: *We are not "normal" and we
know it; it can be fun sometimes but not funny always.*
We tend to be much more sensitive than other people.
Multiple meanings, innuendos, and self-consciousness
plague us. Intensive self-analysis, self-criticism, and the
inability to recognize that we have limits make us
despondent. In fact, most times our self-searching leaves
us more discombobbled than we were at the outset.

The panel of young adult "gifteds" meeting with us
in New York also confirmed some of our feelings, and
provided considerable reassurance and inspiration as
well. Here were four people who had had similar
problems to ours when they were younger and who
were able to rise above these difficulties and become
satisfied, successful, and productive adults. We can't
quote them—it wasn't that kind of formal, taped session
but rather a friendly, personal sharing. We can say,
though, that most of the experiences we have included
here—peer pressures, loneliness, a single-minded

*Project SPARKLE, Norwich, Connecticut Public Schools

9

passion or indecision about which of many interests to pursue—they also experienced. They had bad and great teachers, and all had parents who were extraordinary in their capacity to give freedom, support, and love to those odd birds in the nest.

When you need reassurance that you're not alone in the world and that your problems are not as monumental as you believe them to be, or whether you're in search of inspiration before confronting the system, you may want to reread these next chapters. In the following pages, you'll find many of the most important revelations of our lives.

Listen to us as you would to a friend . . .

INNER PRESSURES

A Burning Desire to Learn?

Lately, I've been telling people, "You know I'm not smart . . . I'm not great. I just have this burning desire to learn!" And that is about the best and simplest way to sum up that entire emotion that occasionally floors me.

I can remember having mad desires to learn how certain things worked, were put together; all from start to finish. Then, I could know and at last be satisfied.

I can remember reading the cereal box as I ate breakfast; all because I had a thirst for literature that drove me to read everything from billboards to bathroom graffiti.

10

On Being Gifted

I used to and still do spend hours in book stores, pacing and picking. I have yet to be able to walk into a book store without any particular literature in mind, browse for a few minutes, decide on a book and purchase it.

Pacing and picking—I wore out the floor trying to decide. The problem is, I want them all. I want to read and discuss, and discuss and read. For what good is knowledge if it is not shared to make another person happy.

How elating it is to talk about a concept which is new to your mental design, a concept which encourages one to develop a different angle of perspective or even a third eye.

In my estimation, it is tastier than the best cuisine, more nutritious than the most carefully grown organic crop. Impartial, well-balanced, definitive intellectual exchange can create the tranquility sought since BB (Before Buddha).

I love to talk and I need to talk. When the appropriate companion is not present and efforts to converse with the person waiting for the bus are futile and de-energizing. I feel like running away.

More often, I become sad out of self-pity. My unconscious takes the fore, relieving my restless stream of thoughts in slumber. I doze and hope to dream of fulfilling my ideal.

Ideal what?

Ideal anything! I have so many unattained ideals I could turn into reality.

━━━━━

About Setting Standards for Yourself?

No one ever told me what to strive for. When I got an excellent paper, the teacher never told me how I could have improved on it or expand the given theme.

They (teachers) were always very pleased to see me earn another eighty or ninety. They always said I was "good" and expected me to continue in that form.

Me, I thought I was nothing. I'd look at my eighty or ninety in disgust. *I always asked myself what is "good." What should I expect of myself?*

I'd heard it said, "the sky's the limit." But, how was I to know that, for I did not have anything to compare it with, the sky was limitless. As far as I could surmise, the ninety was close to the sky—of my English class. Though I made plenty of nineties, they never added up to a one hundred on my final report. I thought, "Was one hundred the sky?" I had come close but never quite touched the blue; at least the one hundred mark was what I thought to be the blue.

I'd come so close with so little effort. I knew my English and history classes were not challenging. I knew all my teachers were not challenging me. I knew their skies were not my skies.

Upon receiving a ninety, I'd think, "This is almost a perfect paper I have, but would a college professor have given me the same grade? Or, are their skies different, higher than those of my teachers?" If so, I should be his student. I knew then that it was time to move on. High school was not the place for me. All this happened when I was fourteen and had only just entered high school as a ninth grader.

I wondered daily about college. How high does one have to go to get nineties at this particular college? At Harvard? Yale? Oxford? Could I reach these heights? How much effort would it take? Just how "good" am I? *Just how smart is smart?* The questions constantly plagued me.

Those questions hatched in succession with no incubating light of an idea to warm their growth into answers. They sat around, miserably peeking for recognition.

Only now are they wobbling to a stand, their wet features drying to down. At this stage of development, another egg has been laid and labelled, "How do I become better than the bestest best?"

▬▬▬

About Your Own Responsibility to Yourself?

The eleventh and twelfth grades were my most enjoyable years. Socially, there was plenty of excitement; academically, well, that could have been better.

The reason the latter was not extremely successful—the former took priority. This is particularly true of the eleventh grade. Because all my close associates went to college, twelfth grade was highly successful. To put it simply, my friends were an obstacle in my academic progress. *I was so hung up in conforming to what they expected of me that I did not take my school work as seriously as I should have.*

On the positive side, twelfth grade was successful because I achieved something that I never dreamed would happen at that stage—becoming gainfully employed.

In looking back on the culmination of events, I am thankful and can say, "I did it my way." I have learned that you only get out of life what you put into it. How true the saying is. I can see where I put miles of effort into my pursuits. I can see where I put little or no effort forth. And the results correspond every time.

That is to say, when I put forth little effort I suffered and vice versa. I cannot blame my teachers totally for not challenging me. I do blame myself for not making school more of a challenge. Consequently, I've missed out on a lot of extras, a lot of knowledge which could have been gotten by reserving one hour a day to read more. Or, one hour a week to spend more time at the library. Yet, I allowed my energies to be spent on frivolous projects which led nowhere, except maybe to a short-lived thrill.

Though I realized learning was a thrill, I suppressed the yearning or transformed it, in some cases even degraded it in order to be accepted by peers. Consequently, frivolities won over.

／■／■／

Are You a Minority Within Our Gifted and Talented Minority?

Our Indian culture views gifted and talented youth in a type of religious manner. For our part, it takes quite a bit of intelligence to understand what goes on around us—such as the religious ceremonies. The elderly people believe you are nothing unless as an Indian you know you *are* an Indian and are fully aware of your culture.

But, in retrospect, we have the same interpretations of various aspects in life, whether it be of old legends or of religious beliefs.

Sometimes I am quite confused over certain things because of my two different cultures. I feel you have to adjust yourself to completely understand society *now*.

Educational opportunities for gifted and talented native Americans are a lot stronger now. There are more chances for higher education at more institutions, but we definitely need an even greater force to educate the rural gifted and talented native American.

Living in a rural area is undoubtedly different from living in an urbanized residence. I don't have much of an opportunity to increase my learning ability. Libraries and various other learning centers are situated in distant places requiring transportation and time for further studying. Yet, living in a rural area does have a basic

15

learning value also, such as studying in secluded places where "city noise" is non-existent or sometimes just studying life itself. We have time and a place to do that without distraction.

Although I feel I have matured quite fast in the last several months since early admission to the local university, my life has not changed much because of my so-called "unique learning needs." Other than that, our school requires the usual classes to be taken in order to graduate with a certain amount of credit hours. This is where kids become bored. We all need a change of environment which goes along with selecting a wider variety of chosen fields. I myself became very depressed when higher educational opportunities were non-existent for students with unique learning needs. In addition, our community also fails to cooperate. *I mean, there are all these organizations helping the underachieving students, when I feel I need help, too!*

The Original Chocolate Cookie Analogy

It seems the only time I write is when things are going down and I can't talk to anybody. And talking in my head gets to be exasperating because I can't ever find a just conclusion. Today is Saturday and I have done absolutely nothing . . . I am just feeling sorry for myself now. I know it and I admit it. That's about the only just and right conclusion that I did come to.

And another thing I just thought of was that I'm

too sensitive at times. At other times an atom bomb in the backyard wouldn't faze me. Mostly the small things eat away at me and the big things that hang most people up—like death, nakedness, loss, sex, appearances, luxuries, possessions—don't faze me one bit.

Today, as I sat in the dark thinking, I closed my eyes and I felt like a cookie in a package. Along with a lot of other chocolate cookies that no one cares about. We're just there among a whole supermarket full of goods. Very seldom do people look on the chocolate cookie shelf. And even fewer people go to the trouble of buying chocolate cookies—they don't sincerely care if we chocolate cookies meet the standards of the rest of the supermarket society.

We're wasted! Wasted like common cookies. Well, speaking on behalf of the chocolate cookie shelves everywhere: "We are not," I repeat, "Not, ordinary, common cookies!" Is there a soul in the world who can appreciate our worth? Will no one accept us? Are we destined to go stale and be wasted for all time? Only the chocolate cookie, God knows!

Frequently we want much more out of life than others—to push to the limit. The lucky ones among us have come to terms with ourselves and already have a feel about where we're going and how to get there.

I Don't Wanna be Human Anymore

Too early in my life, I felt that I didn't want to be human anymore. I didn't want to die, yet, continuing on in the state I was in wasn't hittin' on nothin'.

The hard core fact that life has limitations hit me like a baseball in the eye and I cried. (The baseball accident actually occurred.)

The things that I had not done naturally outweighed those I had. But somehow I knew it didn't take a sip from every cup to know that the next will be the same in that it is different. Somehow I knew, once you had experienced the deepest possible state of sadness, maybe over the death of your dog, the exact same feeling would prevail over the death of your mother. Though the causes differ, the reactions were limited in their degree of expression. I knew this early in the short time I'd lived and it silenced me.

It was as if someone had sounded a gigantic gong in my chest and I was dumbfounded by the vibrations. They still reverberate in my chest.

Yes, once you had laughed as hard as humanly possible for your body to stand, there was no exceeding that. What could I do to change that? There must be something more, a higher degree perhaps? And, I was determined to find that unnamed thing, feel that higher degree.

Until then I'd never heard the phrase "transcend the human condition." But I knew that was what I longed to do. But once I did that, where would I go from there? I asked this even before I explored the question that preceded it.

If I do transcend, are there other degrees or is there just one more? If there is just one more, maybe in its experience there is serenity at the end? Maybe once I've learned the hardest, loudest, longest laugh, there will be peace at the end.

I suppose it could be said that I was not merely yearning to experience the unexperienced, to go beyond the body's limits while yet embodied. And maybe that I was searching for an end to my yearning. I was searching for peace. I was searching for the permanent state of silence I'd experienced upon becoming aware of the limits.

I didn't want to be human anymore. I wanted to travel beyond laughing till I cried.

━━━

Just You and Me

Problems with being gifted? Well, some. I've fortunately outgrown the bullies-in-the-schoolyard stage, not that I didn't have my share (and perhaps more than my share) of problems with them as a child. With age and maturity come newer bullies, infinitely more cunning and resourceful; I'm referring to those teachers who assume that I can handle any amount of homework they choose to give me at any given time. The trouble with these bullies is that you can't run to teacher for help with them. Perhaps you could run to the schoolyard?

␣␣␣␣␣␣␣␣␣␣␣␣␣␣␣␣

Some people are turned off by the amount of recognition I've had; some people assume I'm conceited and untouchable, or impossible to get along with. *They've heard of me but they don't know me in person; they've read the reviews and think they've read the book.* People are prone to jump to conclusions about me solely because of any "gifted" image I may have; some people have already made up their minds about me or decided that I'm not their type. Some people don't think I could ever be interested in their more mundane things like parties and girls.

On the whole, though, I have to confess that I'd rather be a troubled "genius" and a "struggling young writer" than a straight-C student who spends free weekends carrying bags at the A&P. Sacrificing any talent which you may have isn't the way to accomplish anything in life. My life is not without its rewards, obviously (I'm here in the Symposium, and don't you forget it!); I may not get along as well as I'd like to with everyone, but the important thing is do I get along with myself?

Frankly, I'd rather not answer that question at this time, but I guess I'll take a shot at it. You have to, sooner or later.

On the whole, yeah, I guess I do get along with myself. I'm on speaking terms with myself to the point where I can decide what I *want* in life, and I know myself well enough to plan how I might *get* what I want in life. Occasionally, it's more the type of relationship characterized by "Well, no one *else* gets along with you" or the schizoid dialogues like "Well, friend, looks like it's just you and me again." When you get right down to it, I'm all I've got.

And those other guys don't know what they're missing.

／━／━／

PEER PRESSURE

To many with exceptional talents a problem arises concerning their peers and contacts with other people. Of course the gifted student is proud of his powers but his peer group makes it very difficult for him.

People with special gifts get a great deal of attention from the society around them. For me it is not as great a problem as for others simply because I am in my own age group. However, prodding, teasing, and resentment do present themselves as foolish obstacles.

Students in my peer group are jealous about my ability. I do my best to share with them my knowledge and I try to help them whenever possible but all this is to no avail. (Jealousy stirs teasing—which gets to be a drag.)

／━／━／

How's Your Love Life?

If you are a "gifted and talented" student probably

not very good. After all, what is a love life? Intelligent people do not party, drink, or date; they are the ones that stay home and work the calculus problems so that everyone can copy the homework in the morning. Some people don't think that we "gifties" could be interested in mundane things like parties and the opposite sex. Well, we are! That's right, folks—"gifties" enjoy fun things, too!

Even so, don't be afraid to develop your talents because you don't want to be a social outcast. Ponder this thought: you can always catch up socially, but if a talent is dormant too long, it may deteriorate. So don't worry about your social inactivity—it may catch up with you and when it does—watch out!

One problem of being gifted is that kids get jealous of me. My main problem is that kids think of me differently. I absolutely don't want to be considered better than them, and I don't want teachers to think I am better, either. This makes me feel alone and different. I want to feel "with it."

What makes me happy about being gifted . . . I like to be able to do many special activities and I like to be able to catch on fast. *

*Indented quotes above and following are from gifted 4th, 5th and 6th graders in Norwich, Connecticut.

On Being Gifted

— / — / —

Personality Problems—Me?

Although it has taken quite a few years I have begun to understand how to treat people. Being one of the "smarties" isn't easy. Actually, it's on the same wave length to some people as a man with only one leg: it's a social handicap and everyone stares. With myself, I admit, it hasn't been that bad. I know how to deal with people on almost all levels. I can hold an intelligent conversation with the most uneducated person or with someone much more perceptive than myself. (Well, I try hard.) I have friends on every plateau and I enjoy being with all of them. Since our school is quite a small one, I have known and grown up with the same kids. I still get embarrassed when people call me "gifted" (proud grandma) or tease me about my A's (which I do not work hard for) but in all, socially I get along quite well. I get involved with class leadership, American Field Service, and other school functions but I honestly feel people accept me for what I am.

But all that does not mean I am content. I am frustrated so many times with the element of boredom, the lack of evident caring on the teacher's part. *I seem to be in one of those mazes searching for the opening only to crash into walls of glass.*

— / — / —

Sometimes being a gifted kid is embarrassing. For

instance, once I was in Social Studies and I received
a bad mark and the teacher expected a better mark
from me . . . Once in a while you just feel like
saying "go away" or something.

—————

Caught in the Middle

As I sit in a classroom of a smalltown high school, I
am listening to the teacher begin a lecture for the day.
He asks a question regarding the assigned homework,
chapter 25 in our book. I raise my hand and respond
correctly to his query. He continues to ask questions and
I continue to answer them. After a couple of rounds I
begin to look around sheepishly to see if anyone else has
his hand raised. No one does so I answer again. I hear
annoyed mutterings from my classmates. I just know
they're thinking, "She thinks she knows everything." So
in a futile effort to conform and satisfy them, I sink
down in my seat just a little and let the rest of the
questions slide by. The teacher becomes angry that no
one has read the assignment and feels he must repeat the
chapter. And another day is wasted.

So goes it, and unfortunately, too often. As a result,
I do not feel challenged nor do I attempt to be when I
find myself in such a class. One alternative, which in my
school is extremely limited, is to sign up for those courses
which are designed for people planning to major in that
specific area. But alas, not enough teachers, nor enough

money in the budget for books or supplies. So suffer, kid!

━ ⁄ ━ ⁄

What I like is when teachers are glad you're gifted and are willing to stick up for you. But it makes you feel down low when people tease you for being gifted.

━ ⁄ ━ ⁄

The Outcast

My earliest remembrance of being outcast was in the fourth grade. I was a member of the modern dance club, a very prestigious position. The modern dance girls were looked upon as cute, ladylike, and a bit more mature and responsible than their classmates. But that aspect didn't please me. It wasn't the main thrust behind my involvement in the club—creation was.

For me, all living, breathing, eating, and dreaming was enveloped in the art of dance, the love of creating. I was an indefatigable dancer. One day my teacher said I was very good. This comment was made to my mother at a PTA meeting. I was taken aback when she told me of his approval. Somehow everyone, the whole fourth grade, found out.

To the whole fourth grade, though, another girl was the best. She was more popular than I and that alone made her the best at everything; the group measured her ability, and as far as they were concerned, she could do no wrong.

It was true that she was a poised, attractive, self-confident individual who made fair grades. In my case, I possessed some of the same qualities but was one of the "smarties." "Smarties" were not popular with the majority. They were very often cast out.

Because of her popularity, no one dared compete with her. Such actions would only get you a bloody nose, dirty looks or definite ostracization. She was an established figure and it was comfortable that way.

But me, I danced for my own enjoyment and spiritual fulfillment. I had no confidence, was only of average appearance and, as I mentioned, made excellent grades.

I was, at the very least, shunned. At the most, I was hated simply because of my scholastic record.

It's a rotten feeling to have people just turn against you when they find out you're gifted. But just the same, they are just jealous and wish they were in your shoes.

Paranoia

For many years, I was plagued by paranoia. I felt

inferior because I was told too many times in the wrong company that I was smart.

The wrong company I am referring to is my peers. And adults were always doing the telling, the complimenting. At times I wanted to shrink away and never have to look at another human being again. I didn't want to be picked out as special. *I hated being at the head of the class. Naturally, my peers hated me too. But the self-hatred was more intense.*

Eventually, I began to withdraw more and more each day. I wouldn't talk. I ate very little. I stayed in my room too much. I did have friends, but I couldn't match their standards all the time. Though I tried desperately to make the same jokes, talk the same slang, enjoy the same pastimes, it didn't always run smoothly. I'd hit bumps and just have to admit to myself just how phony it was. It was a bore. I got bored with my very closest friends and that left no one to confide in.

It eventually degenerated into a very bad situation. I began to see less of my friends and I thought that they were talking about me behind my back. I imagined that they were jealous and I know I was right to a certain degree.

━ ╱ ━ ╱ ━ ╱

. . . And then they will tease me about it. I try to ignore it, but then I have no one to turn to . . .

━ ╱ ━ ╱ ━ ╱

27

PRESSURES FROM TEACHERS

You have read in the section above that praise and extra attention from teachers is frequently one of the causes of our rejection by our peers. But often our peers get their cues when our teachers begin to reject us. This often happens when an instructor feels threatened by the exceptional student. In my school this takes the form of neglect. The teacher does not fill my needs because he will not devote extra time to me and often totally ignores my suggestions.

Often, instructors, though not actually threatened, feel that the gifted student has had enough recognition and therefore bypass him. Many times one of my teachers has preferred to work extremely hard with his favorite remedial workshop student than to talk to me. This sort of behavior has caused me to doubt my priorities concerning education.

These rejections, resentments, and prejudices create unnecessary pressures on exceptional students. The following few pages contain our commentaries on the social and psychological problems caused by the pressure of some unnecessarily resentful teachers we have known. To balance the record, you will find in the next chapter how we have responded to different treatment.

Who's on Our Side?

Occasionally teachers seem to be foes rather than

allies. Unfortunately, many times teachers are on an ego trip, preferring to help slower students so that they might appear to be all-powerful and all-knowing.

If a student happens to learn rapidly or already has a knowledge of the subject from prior exposure, the teacher develops a deep resentment for the child.

In my case, I had a teacher of algebra who developed this type of resentment. I understood the material because of previous contact with the subject. I seldom missed problems on tests, homework or on the board; when I did, I caught his wrath.

I don't know the psychological reasons; I only know this situation shouldn't exist.

=/=/

From Busy Work to the Rare Educator

I have had many difficult experiences because I was able to grasp subject matter quickly. Often, a teacher becomes so involved with teaching students who learn slowly that he gives "busy work" to the student who has already caught on. *Crossword puzzles and scrabble just don't seem to satisfy my educational needs!* Other teachers ignore these situations completely, while some take to openly hostile behavior. Many teachers resent students who are bright and punish them with remarks in class and with poor scores. Consequently, the student becomes bitter and often becomes a behavior problem.

I've seen this happen many times and yet could do

little or nothing. Finally, there is an educator who acknowledges your "hunger" for material and provides incentive, true learning experiences, or even refers you to another teacher or introduces you to a new method of learning. This is the educator who provides enough incentive for one to stay in school. At least, in my case it did. It is a pity that there are so few teachers like this!

I Can Do Something

It's very difficult for me with teachers who ignore and resent me but I have found a few things which I can do.

I have found peace in the knowledge that I am not the only person in the world in this situation. I do my best to maintain tranquility between myself and the teacher. Another thing I have learned to realize is that similar situations will occur in the world I will live in. I will have to cope with these also.

Soon the problem will fade from my life and I hope I will not remember these trying times. This period of unnecessary rejection and resentment causes large problems for the individual. I hope it can and will be stopped.

I am in an unusual situation, a sophomore in

college at age 15. One question I am often asked is how I fit in socially, and I would like to respond here.

Basically, I feel I am at my intellectual level, and it seems to me that a "social level" does not take second place to that. Also, it seems that one's social level follows, more or less, from one's intellectual level. I cannot substantiate that, except that my experience has shown this to be true.

Sure, there is the shock on people's faces as they say "You're how *old*?" and other superficial things such as being underage for many activities in which your older friends participate. All the people I know who have skipped grades (a disproportionate number due to the particular program I am in) have been extremely satisfied.

Anxiety is a difficult thing to cope with; leaving one's peers behind can be traumatic for some people. But I feel this is a case of what you don't do can hurt you. You may be adequately challenged intellectually now, but if not, you may want to consider seriously skipping a grade or two. I would highly recommend it.

━━━

HOW TO COPE

If you are like us, you know that when you exhibit extraordinary abilities, other people tend to exaggerate them. In their minds, you become a "genius" and/or an eccentric.

While your work may be exceptional, you may simply not be able to achieve at the level on which others may expect to constantly operate. With the passing of time, you may find that your performance is farther and farther from what is expected of you. Pursuing one course of action, you may attempt to do things beyond your reach. At some point, you will probably tell yourself that you have no talent, which is, of course, untrue. Your mind will vacillate between believing that you are a genius and believing that you are a failure. Neither being true, you may become extremely depressed or confused and your opinion of yourself will begin to break down.

What you must try to do is to realize that you are talented to some extent and not attempt to accomplish the impossible. Take yourself seriously, but not too seriously. Everyone, even the gifted student, has limits. You can still reach for high goals, but if you cannot attain them, you must somehow try to learn to live with yourself, knowing that you have done the best that you possibly could. How? Well, since we are all "unique," we must all do it our own best way—and the only rule we can think of for everyone is to keep trying, fighting those slumps. Having a positive opinion of yourself, psyching yourself up, can renew the confidence you need to get yourself out of a depression. You have to have had some triumphs here and there. Remember them!

You must try your hardest and then learn to be satisfied with your achievements. You must accept,

32

develop, and have pride in your potential. You *must* be considerate to your fellow human beings and not impose your internal conflicts and/or egocentricities on them. Don't dig yourself a hole: reach out.

To relate to others is impossible without first understanding yourself, but don't make that an exclusive activity. Some gifted people, aware of their talents, become extremely contemptuous of others less well endowed than themselves. Bright people like you are more perceptive and can usually understand other people quite easily. But you (and we) often speak and write in a "hinting" style. By this, we mean giving only the briefest germ of an idea and then assuming that everyone will catch the gist of what you are talking about. That's how you can be misunderstood; you can change that if you stop to think about it.

Many kids have been able to deal with peers by learning to be more explicit and by relaxing their formal manners. You don't have to copy anybody else or make a big thing about learning the current jargon if it doesn't interest you; but you can loosen up a little and be low-key and talk about or listen to somebody else's interest for a change.

On the other hand, a lot of talented kids have no formal manners to abandon. These kids, in addition to the ones who truly don't care about peer sentiments, are generally the most contented. If you are among them, you are lucky, because you won't have qualms about your unusual abilities and will be free to push on regardless.

If, on the other hand, you often feel that life is futile, you have already accomplished everything that you possibly can, that you might just commit suicide (we often think that way, some of us), the best quick advice we can think of is to go to sleep. On awakening, you will realize that there always is an alternative. Don't laugh; we mean it!

Here are a few more simple home remedies we have tried.

A Whole New World

When your mind feels restrained and boxed in on four sides with superficial teachers, boring school days and no challenge whatsoever, I recommend the world's best antidote. This secret remedy is simply reading. Books truly open up whole new worlds. When your own life becomes dull and monotonous, you can easily delve into someone else's through books. I can throw myself, mind and body, into a good book and watch reality slip away. There is so much to be learned—limitations at school shouldn't stop you. Remember, books are a great place to visit, and you know, sometimes I wouldn't mind living there.

Coping with Tension

Tension often builds in the bodies of gifted students. These tensions must be relaxed and I have tried and found many ways to do so.

Of course, one of the most favorite pastimes is to recline on a soft couch and fall asleep, but this does become monotonous, boring, and dull. I have learned to become deeply interested in a subject to where my mind thinks of nothing else. My love for this hobby becomes insatiable.

I took up stamp collecting at the age of 9 and I collected with fervor until I was 13. I then began to collect irregularly; by the age of 16 I had lost my interest in philatelics. I became quite an expert in the stamp field—I could learn no more about it. I wished only to collect the unique, expensive, ancient stamps and I became frustrated. I still have my stamps and wait for the urge to return to them.

At 15 I started sailing and I still love it. The only problem is finding a boat, but at least I know how to handle it.

At 16 I decided stamps and sailing were hobbies I could not enjoy anytime I wished. I had lost the fervor of collecting and had realized I might never possess a sailboat. Secondly, I felt my creativity was being hampered because there is really no creative thinking in these two hobbies.

Finally, I got hold of a camera and to this day it is my favorite hobby. Photography is never the same. Stamp collecting has its "fill in the space" and sailing its knowledge, but photography is all creativity.

Now I grab my camera, walk outside, and shoot. I

get excited waiting for my pictures, hoping that they turn out well.

Photography is stimulating. Every time the camera shutter opens, the picture is always slightly different. My mind is blank to the world; my prime connection with reality is the view-finder. I relax.

Every time I feel depressed I work on one of my many hobbies and I soon forget my miseries. I sometimes find they were really not problems at all.

—·—·—·

Commitment vs. Potential

I have unusually been one of the best students and one of the best musicians in my vicinity. Many times I have wondered how I'd compare to people from all over the country or even people all over the world. Not knowing just how strong I am in certain areas has given me difficulties in planning my future.

So I've decided to follow up on my strongest aptitudes in an environment where other people of similar talents would be. I am going to a top-rated conservatory for music. If after a year I find that I am not among the top in this group I will try one of my other options. *I have convinced myself that I can be happy in any discipline, once I commit myself.*

—·—·—·

SUMMARY

In this section of the book we have discussed problems of peer rejection, teacher influences, social values, problems of age disparities and how these can lead to emotional troubles. Some ways of dealing successfully with these difficulties have also been explored.

We have often felt desperately alone and caught up in ourselves. We hope that the experiences we have described can provide solace and constructive advice when you feel oppressed by pressures, real or imagined.

For what it's worth, when we wonder whether or not being gifted is worth the extreme depression, excruciating sensitivity, inability to relate, and/or tendency to over-analyze, all of us vote "yes." The elation that comes with rapid comprehension, the wide range of understanding open to us, the self-satisfaction that comes from developing a talent and the ability to empathize easily do make the "lows" bearable. So we hope that you will come to feel that way, too.

Chapter II

People Who Helped

IN the last chapter, we concentrated on ourselves and our peers with an occasional nod to the adults in our lives. Now, we'd like to talk more about those people who have most influenced us—our parents, our teachers, and in a few cases, other adult mentors. These are the closest relationships we have developed with the adult world; we titled this chapter "People Who Helped" because, by and large, that is the heart of the matter. Without them, where would we be? Who would we have to talk to? Who else identifies those vague early stirrings of ours and helps us to know what they mean, or provides the outlets, and sets us on our first steps toward reaching that potential we talk about so much.

Not that these relationships are trouble free, not at all. We aren't always paragons of patience and virtue; neither are they. We don't avoid that in telling you about our experiences either. We also explore here the kinds of help we found to be most vital and describe

39

what kind of people kindly gave it. *We hope that you have at least one person like those we describe in your life; if you don't, start looking.* For any educators looking over our shoulders, we want you to know the sort of persons we value. You can reward us by rewarding and encouraging them; we need more. To some of us, it's a matter of life and death!

We would like to salute the "helper" of one of our young adult panel members who for two summers running provided the funds to send him to a school for conductors in Europe on the condition that his identity remain anonymous. Now, that's caring!

OUR PARENTS

Opening up Opportunities

How did my parents help me grow? They attempted and still give me all the opportunities for development possible.

My father has gotten jobs for me, and he even enrolled me in a course at Louisiana State University when I was 13. I really did not want to attend but my father urged me on. I found I really liked to study and to learn. Although I felt out of place with college students, I didn't mind; my entire entity was too busy with the course.

With this course I got a jump on everyone. I learned that I was exceptional and I learned to accept it.

My parents recognized this too and sent me to an exceptional high school.

My parents sweated to send me to a private school and are still now sweating so that I might have other opportunities. For them and for me, there is no price on education. It's worth it.

At Catholic High I have become involved with many clubs and have taken thorough advantage of all the academic opportunities available there.

Because of my "giftedness" and also because I was a fat little kid, I had not enjoyed much of a social life. But Catholic High changed that. Now no one can spot me from the rest of the crowd unless, of course, they know me. I have become socially acceptable. I have not conformed; I have refined myself. I'm no longer nervous or shy. Believe me, the school makes a hell of a lot of difference.

In addition to making that school possible for me through their sacrifices, my parents have made me work in fields in which I had no interest, such as construction. Even though I disliked the work, I learned how to adapt and how to survive. My parents let me do things I want to do, too. I am free and independent. They talk to me like an adult; they trust me, and I respect them. The only differences we have had are those of degree; they sometimes harped too much on achievement. They wanted awards; not me. I was indifferent.

What would I do if I were a parent of a gifted and talented child? I don't even know what I would do if I were a regular parent!

41

On Values—Pro

My family has valued education and has strong interests in art, literature and music. Because we are close, I've tried to emulate my parents. It is by imitating them, rather than from their telling me what to do, that I've developed a passion for learning and a compulsion to work in an organized manner. But I strongly believe that because of their love and affection, my parents gave me the self-esteem which is an essential element in constructive thinking.

Perhaps this is a good place to pass on the comments of one of our adult panel friends on peer and parent relationships. He said he worked out peer group conflicts by becoming a good fighter and a good stickball player, but that he was never tempted to give up "the life of the mind" to gain peer acceptance. He was surrounded by so much love at home that he never felt the need.

On Values—Con

My parents never sat down and talked to me about what is right and what is wrong, but I know how they feel from the way they talk. For instance: "Catholicism

42

is the best religion; premarital sex is wrong; America is the greatest country on earth; and members of ethnic minorities are alright, but don't marry one." I don't believe any of that. My parents raised me in the belief that if I were continually exposed to these ideas, I would naturally believe in them. They were so wrong it's not funny.

Unlike most of the innocents I know, I started questioning society's values at a very tender age. I finally came to the conclusion that Catholicism was another version of a three-ring circus, sex is fine if the girl doesn't get pregnant, our country isn't that cool, and I just recently broke up with a black guy with whom I had been going steady for a year and a half.

It's not unusual for gifted kids to question values at an early age. *My favorite word is "Why?"* It's only natural that I should ask about values and morals. Nonetheless, it causes lots of problems to have different values from these people on whom you are dependent and who have claims on you. But I have to feel free to make up my own mind and I do.

/ — / — /

Earning Independence

My parents have not approved of many of the things I've done to improve my education. These include taking days and even weeks off from my school to study or practice my musical instruments. They've consented nonetheless, because I have proved to them that

I'm achieving. I'm my school's valedictorian and the New York Youth Symphony's principal bassoonist.

The same goes for the principal of my school. I wanted to concentrate on practicing but a course requirement in chemistry got in the way. So I got him to agree to allow me the time off if I passed the chemistry final exam. I then took two weeks off to prepare, passed the exam, and was home free. It shook everybody up a little, but no one could argue with me after that.

My younger sister often feels that she has to copy my achievements. She sometimes shouts, "Just because you get straight A's doesn't mean I have to get them!" I understand the pressure she feels, but I can't go over-board over it because I think she's cheating herself. She's bright, too, but she's lazy. The thing of it is, in our house, it's normal to be ahead of yourself—we all are, or have been, including my parents.

Conceivably, though, some younger children could find that too much and react in extremes, perhaps becoming indifferent and not achieving at all or maybe becoming challenged to the point where they would do anything to outperform their older sibling.

The Artist's Agent

At one point in my life, I was undecided about where I wanted to go and what I wanted to do with my studies. Going to school from day to day had about as much fulfillment as brushing my teeth or going to bed. I listened to instructors with half an ear.

To break out of this drudgery and boredom, I turned to my art. *My parents noticed my ability and were behind me one hundred percent, neither pushing nor aloof. (They never have, in fact, hindered, but have given what they could.)*

As I grew more restless in public school, I decided to get out. My mother did the field work in finding out about a very special art school in town. That school changed my whole outlook on education. I dearly loved my art and for the first time became interested in learning in general. If it had not been for my parents giving me the support I needed, I would have continued to deteriorate in a mechanical classroom setting.

There is almost always easy communication about problems among us; this is, I think, one of the most important facets of my relationship with my parents. Patience, especially on my mother's part, understanding, interest and, most of all, support and exposure to many stimuli have helped me to achieve my goals.

Kids go through some very difficult times in their early teens and that seems to be a crucial turning point. They are often offended when their parents interfere. To many "gifted and talented" students, privacy is a prized possession, and if they are deprived of it, they can become irritable and moody.

As a parent, I would try to create an atmosphere

where my children were as unscheduled as possible, where they could have time of their own. Exposure to books, theatre, special classes, cultural events—many things—should be available to them as often as possible.

Many teachers fail to detect our hidden needs; this is where parents are of the utmost importance.

———

The Youth Worker

I was given responsibilities at an early age, being the eldest of five children. I always tried to set an example for my younger brothers and sister. My mother told me to make the best of life, to stand up for what I believe, and to respect everyone else for their own beliefs.

I've always wanted to take part in just about everything, but my father seemed to be more interested in my academic achievements rather than my social involvement in school. Because we live on a reservation, I also had transportation problems which held me back from being too active.

The most important thing to me is that my parents and I can talk to each other truthfully. We can point out faults in each other. My mom worked as a supervisor in the Neighborhood Youth Corps in Isleta and was involved with high school students. She can easily communicate with them and they can confide in her. She really cares about young people and their problems. I feel that this has helped, too, in my relationships with my parents.

To parents of gifted kids, I would say, "Be very patient!" My parents need to be patient with me because I always have something to do. I am also a scatterbrain. It takes money, too, for it seems like I always need money for this and that. Last, but not least, I would love my child—because we're all gifted one way or another!

▬▬

My Goals/Their Goals

My parents always encouraged me to strive for the highest goals that I could possibly obtain; yet, they were always genuinely sympathetic if the goals I had set were not realized. Their love and understanding always made everything so easy. My goals became their goals. They gave advice, but never made it look like they were "enlightening" me. They are the easiest people in the world to talk to—because they *appreciate* me and I them. *My parents are my best friends: they are always there—when I need them or not. But parents can be the worst critics: most of the time this is most helpful. But sometimes it just plain hurts!*

▬▬

Cultural Exposure

How have my parents helped in my growth and development? They exposed me to different cultural activities, to many kinds of people and situations. They gave me a home with books, music, movies, and the like; they stressed academics. Most of all, they have watched over me and come whenever I needed them, always with good humor and affection. I was encouraged to pursue any of my interests. Though I have never set "goals" for myself and doubt that I ever shall, I cannot imagine my family not backing me.

We have easy communication and a sense of humor with each other. They are among my best friends; I seek and trust their advice over any and all counsel.

Were I to have a gifted child, I would find schools where my child could develop; I would allow her to pursue any of her interests and would attempt to foster them only if my child wanted to do so. She would not be pushed at an early age and would remain with her family, hopefully with children and friends of her own age.

A Sense of Responsibility

My parents instilled in me a sense of responsibility and the initiative to seek out and explore that which interested me. They've always encouraged me to be open-minded, and have supported any interest or endeavor that would add to my cultural, intellectual and emotional growth, such as travel, art and music lessons, films, and books.

They hindered me at times by often expecting too much of me. By being perfectionists, my parents made me feel inadequate and frustrated if I was not constantly performing at my best.

For the most part, my relationship with my parents is an extremely warm and close one. They are extremely concerned with understanding me and being sympathetic to my needs (whether they be intellectual or emotional). They strongly desire that I be a person independent of themselves, and they acknowledge that my expectations, goals, and beliefs are often different from theirs.

If I were a parent, I would try to be aware of my child's needs, and how best to meet them. Being the parent of a "gifted and talented" child, I would have to be especially sensitive to the hardships that giftedness can cause.

As far as growth and development of giftedness, my parents did not help at all because they did not know I was "gifted." Therefore, I developed like everyone else, with typical parental guidance.

As yet, I have not set many long-term goals except to get the most education possible, and my parents are all for that.

Probably the most important facet of our relationship is our mutual respect of each other's privacy. We are not a very close family and in effect we each do as we please without interference.

I think the most important thing for a gifted —especially an exceptionally gifted—child is to develop socially in a normal way. Of equal importance is satisfying his curiosity and meeting his educational needs. This implies exploration of all sorts. These two things are the only two that I would necessarily do for a gifted child because in these areas their needs go beyond the requirements of normal children.

——*

The Gift of Independence

My parents were very supportive and helped me get materials to learn. They have always had faith in me and never pushed me, though they were proud of all my achievements. As for hindering, they didn't. Ever. They were willing to let me be my own person and never tried to make me fit their idea of what I should be. So I would treat a gifted child like any other child. I would help him when he needed it and let him alone when that seemed best. Naturally, he would be different from me, but in these ways his needs would be the same.

——*

On "Not Pushing"

I have benefitted most by my parents' warmth and affection, especially in my earliest years. Also, they set an example for me, as they are both industrious and have diverse interests.

My parents did not push me at all! They let me do my work alone. *They didn't refuse to help when I asked, but did not offer to help me go beyond what I needed to know.* For example, before I entered school, they didn't attempt to teach me to read. My grandparents had given my parents pre-school instruction which led to their skipping grades, which they both found socially upsetting. This is the reason for their not wanting me to be precocious with all the resultant nonacceptance by peers.

They did always try to interest me in the arts, music, literature and sports—my interest in science came from my uncle—but only to the extent that a layman might become involved. Apparently this was enough to stir my curiosity. I might have started to work hard when I was younger, but I could hardly read when I was eight! Of course, it is also possible that had they "pushed" me, I could have been turned off early, too.

On balance, I'd probably do the same things as my parents, and leave my child to his own inventions as much as possible.

=—=—=/

The Role Models

My parents were most helpful to me by serving as excellent role models, especially my mother, who has expanded her learning by holding many different kinds of jobs. She has been everything from an English major to a chemist to the director of an acting troupe in post-war

Germany to a medical librarian to an economics librarian to the head of a data bank. And each time she has changed jobs, she has jumped into a field she knew very little about. The latest jump, to the data bank, is the wildest; she knew almost nothing about computers when she transferred there, but she's learning as she goes.

Reading and literary discussions were always a big part of our household. Anything serious I read, I could be pretty sure Mom would have read or at least would want to hear about. And her own learning behind the scenes has never stopped for a minute. She shares her latest "kick," myths and anthropology, with us so we all get educated at the same time.

I will never be able to know how my parents hindered me, since I don't know what kind of person I would be if they had brought me up differently. One possible negative area in our relationship is the heavily authoritarian structure of our home. Dad always makes the major decisions; we can have or do almost anything we want, but he makes the decisions.

I do regret that my intelligence was always challenged so traditionally. Books were and are the staff of our life, but I never tried many other disciplines, such as engineering or art.

Easy communication was certainly the norm in our household, but with an important qualifying condition: everyone respects each other's privacy and independence. Even as little children, no one ever pried into what my sister and I were doing; curiosity, yes, and willingness to listen and help if that was asked for. But otherwise we were free to go our own ways. And often all four of us did go different ways, so meals could be a little off-schedule. Usually, however, we tried to wait for the last person to arrive home for dinner, and Sunday night was off-limits for going out. Meals became an important time for sharing.

Above all, I respect the way my parents have raised me because they have always respected me.

If I were the mother of a "gifted and talented" child, I would give him or her all the room in the world to explore as many different creative areas as I could. But I would never force him or her to follow any particular bent which he or she did not naturally care about. My child would have every encouragement possible, but I would respect that person as an independent human being with his or her own rights.

───

OUR TEACHERS

We have talked about what we don't like or resent in our teachers. Now, let's turn to those instructors who have given us help, guidance, and inspiration. For a start, here are some of the qualities the *sparkle* students look for. And so do we:

───

ON BEING GIFTED

Teacher's Best Qualities

Understanding toward gifted kids

Has a sense of humor

Doesn't expect you to be right always, or expect you
to be on a 15-year-old level

Doesn't restrict your imagination

Teaches in a manner that is fun, not always out of
the boring textbooks

Helps you when you want. Doesn't make you feel
like you're the worst student because you are
gifted but don't understand things

Makes you think: it's easy to learn out of a text, but
if other learning methods are used, it's sometimes harder

━━━━

In addition to having a comprehensive understanding of the subject matter, we think the teacher
of the gifted should be sensitive to our unique emotional
needs.

━━━━

Starting with the second grade and on through high
school, there have been nine teachers I've admired. I
admired them because their own strength and natural
rapport with students in turn demanded our respect.
Kindness, sensitivity, and intelligence were among their
many qualities and virtues. Most importantly, they

made each student feel significant, as if each one of us had a part of them in reserve. You knew they cared. With all their other responsibilities, they always took time out to personally talk with you, to discuss problems, and to offer suggestions.

It was these qualities that made me look forward to school. *Often, I took refuge in a teacher's understanding and continue to do so.* I could not handle the rejecting attitudes of my peers.

Because I was a good student, both in conduct and grades, teachers were more personable with me. Had I not received this attention, I would probably not have exercised my potential and active participation would have become unthought of.

I had a fantastic teacher in the sixth grade who really just forced me to think on my own. He challenged me always—I loved every minute of it! Learning was an exciting thing and consequently I became an excited person.

His advice and counseling spurred my interest in community affairs. Thanks to his initial concern, things are being done!

The kind of teacher I have now is a kind of person that's funny, a person that tries to do fun things with the class. A person that is nice to the class, and strict only when she has to be. I think teachers should teach in a fun way instead of a way like a dull way. I wouldn't like a teacher that was really mean and didn't have any fun in her.

On Being Gifted

There have been quite a few teachers who have inspired and challenged me through the years. The one who impressed me the most was my zoology teacher. Because I am a science fanatic, I found the usual course matter trivial and quite easy. Although this class may have been fulfilling to the majority of the class, it was not for me.

The teacher saw my situation and gave me additional work to do, including referencing, dissecting various animals, and setting up practicals. Since it was necessary (and not difficult) for me to do the routine class work also, I came during my free time and before and after school. Seeing that I hated to lose access to the science room after the course was completed, this inspirational teacher asked me to come during any free time to help him with his classes as a "zoology aide." I can do any work there now which is a current interest of mine.

Qualities I Look for in a "Good Teacher"

Someone who can mix work with pleasure
Someone who is interested
Someone that understands my advantages and
    disadvantages of being gifted
Someone that understands that I am not perfect
Someone that helps me make up my work

A *Little Approval*

I suppose everyone first loves their kindergarten teacher, either out of necessity, fear, or some other motivation. And I was no exception. So, excluding her, I would say my second grade teacher was the one I loved most. I didn't love her because she smelled good or looked pretty or was like a guardian angel; though she was all of the latter. I loved her because she made me feel significant.

I was a good student; all I wanted to do was please the teacher and I suppose that attitude still exists in me though to a lesser degree. Proof of my eagerness to please Miss S. is evident on the third finger of my right hand: a writer's corn. I used to run back to school following lunch to make it in time to practice handwriting. Capital "N's" gave me the worst problems. Right along with "N's" were "Z's," "K's," and "G's." Determined to make my letters perfect, I held my fat, black number two lead pencil so tightly and pressed so hard, that a corn developed.

The degree of devotion to pleasing my instructors has not diminished with time. I laugh to think that I actually interrupted my good sleep, upset my nerves and busted my brains to impress six people—six people who didn't devote half as much time and energy to my schooling as I did to hear an approving tone in their voice. This is not to say they were shirking their duty. I realize that some teachers, though devoted as nuns,

57

have too many home and family obligations to adequately meet the needs of every individual student. In addition, it is humanly impossible to meet my ideal, no matter how ideal the environmental circumstances.

I would have loved one of those teachers to recognize me and ask, "What are you thinking?" How I would have loved for my teacher to ask, whether out of genuine concern or not, "What's on your mind?" or to write me a pass to the library that would turn me loose there. Instead, I was called on to answer a question that I could not have cared less about, because it was hers, not mine.

▬▬▬

I would like Teachers:

To be funny
To be understanding
To be friendly
To be serious sometimes
To be always ready, up to it, ready to go
To always be smiling
To always be happy
To laugh when something is not funny but you
     meant it to be
To be direct
To not be demanding

▬▬▬

Setting Standards

After spending a week as a kindergarten student —assigned to the afternoon session because I was a little older and, thus, didn't need naps anymore—the teacher, the school psychologist and the principal conferred with my parents and decided that since I could read and had ability, first grade would be a better placement for me. Certain stipulations were agreed upon: I was to go home for lunch and both my parents and the school would carefully monitor my progress.

Everyone was pleased with the decision, but I was a little irked. I was taking psychological tests while my class toured the buildings and I hadn't gotten to fingerpaint, a standard kindergarten activity.

My first grade teacher was thorough and she maintained the same standards for me as for the other students. She knew I could read but she expected me to participate in reading group and complete my workbook, too. She spent extra time teaching me paperfolding and the fine art of tying my cap under my chin. She would not accept carelessly done papers nor take for granted that I "knew it all." A specific incident I remember is writing words with the "ar" sound. I wrote "par" and she asked me to use it in a sentence which I did. She then accepted my response. As an only child, I really hadn't had many experiences playing group games and participating in physical activities. The teacher recognized this, and encouraged my mother to teach me to jump rope and catch and throw balls. What

I'm trying to say is that as a five-year-old gifted child I was like any other child. I needed to have standards imposed upon me so that I could develop the habits that are necessary for successfully continuing my education.

I had a wonderful math and English teacher in sixth grade. She was an older nun of whom I wasn't fond at the time. We used to laugh and joke about the talks she gave to help us realize the importance of learning. I can still hear her saying about English, "The public schools may be throwing grammar out the window, but we aren't!" and about math, "When I was in school, they never taught us why we did anything, we just had to do it. You're going to learn why." And we did.

These two beliefs led her to teach me math and English fundamentals which enabled me to breeze through my next three years of these subjects. When I started going to a public school, I was one of the very few students who understood what they were doing in math and knew the difference between a noun and a verb.

One area in which I've been especially lucky is French. I've had four French teachers and they've all been super. I didn't take first year French in seventh grade, as the school I attended didn't offer it. The public schools had a rule that in seventh grade you take first year French and in the eighth grade you take the second year course. No exception. That left me up the proverbial creek. We visited the local junior high principal. He

60

worked out a deal whereby I could get a tutor through the public school system to learn first year French.

My tutor was great. With her help I learned one year of French in three months. My teacher for the next two years expected a lot of me. She never let me get away with average work. I had to do above average work. She also cared about the emotions of her students. Sometimes we just put our books away and talked, as when one of our fellow French students was strangled by her mother.

In high school, I had a strict French teacher. She made me do the same work as everyone else. She was a good teacher and everyone learned in her class. My present French teacher stresses initiative. I'm taking French independent study, and she insists that I choose 50% of my work. She knows her subject matter well. Not only does she speak beautiful French, she knows about the cultures of all French speaking peoples.

One of my junior high English teachers needs to be mentioned because of a humanistic but unconventional approach to discipline. He sent me to the office once for participating in a game of "throw the white spray can cap." When he talked to me, he suggested that I write my feelings about the class and incident. I did and he responded in writing. After a few "back-and-forths," I had vented my feelings and grew a little from reading his reactions.

In a high school of 1,800 students, I really did not expect to receive very much individual attention; in fact, my whole attitude was pretty bad. My counselor visited with me about my ability and about the importance of really working in high school. His interest in me persisted until I really began to believe that I could go to him with any problem or question. He has assisted me in various applications for scholarships and has written countless recommendations for me. He has offered guidance in college selection but most of all, he accepts me as a person who sometimes needs help and sometimes needs conversation. In all my conversations with him, I've always felt that the decisions were mine but he'd provide as much information as he could.

The high school in general has assisted me by giving moral support. The teachers and administration care about students as individuals. They are open to change and new ideas.

One of my worst areas is science. Whenever I hear that awful word, I cringe. Somehow, all of my science courses have failed to teach me very much. I equated science with confusion and failure. With this attitude I walked into chemistry. I didn't expect to learn much, but it's supposed to be a good course to take. My teacher explains what he's saying and makes sure everyone understands before he goes on. I'm beginning to think that maybe I'll learn something and learn to like chemistry. Without this man's patience, I may have never changed my attitude about science and thus never given myself a chance to learn anything in this area.

The Teacher As Critic

When you're wandering around through elementary school as I was, vaguely aware that you're different in a superior sense and able to read the "Dick and Jane" books before you even entered school, you may not have much sense of direction. You know that something is with you, something is following you throughout life. What can be invaluable is someone outside taking an interest in your case, and telling you about the potential of extraordinary capabilities you may not know you have.

I was born (prematurely) wanting to be a writer, but I didn't know it until I was about twelve. Writing is a dreadful thing to deal with in an educational sense because no one can really sit you down and teach you how to write. Getting background information and really knowing about your subject is great; studying what other authors have done is even better. And good, tough criticism is certainly invaluable. But when it comes right down to it, if you're not a writer inside you, you may never be one for real. It's a cruel pastime, finding that out, but first you've got to try.

I had a really skilled teacher who gave me an absolutely incredible, brilliant ninth grade English education. Before that, he'd made a few trips over to the elementary school and helped me with my poetry as early as fourth grade. My high school class of '76 has been watched and guided from elementary school on and there are an awful lot of us, modesty aside, who are really good people. *Hearing other symposium participants complain about their treatment in the public school system has made me realize how comparatively excellent my own has been.* And to this day, that English teacher remains my number one teacher of all time.

My great-aunt, pushing seventy but only recently retired from teaching English and drama at a Rochester high school where she has earned thousands of fervent admirers, would still be called "gifted and talented." With me, she has almost single-handedly channeled my interest in writing into actual performance. Along with my family, which is a highly literate one, she showed me that if you're willing to work a little, having an exceptional skill can open up doors and outlooks onto this absolutely fantastic world of limitless imagination and boundless possibilities—what can only be described as staggering potential. Infinite diversity in infinite combinations, to fall back on *Star Trek* for a bit.

—————

SUMMARY

In summary, we realize that personal relationships can provide a wonderful experience of closeness and understanding. This may not come about without special recognition for and insight into our needs. Loving parents meet those needs, even where they do not or have not perceived our "giftedness"; but recognition and help from our teachers is crucial to us. *These people who give of themselves, of their time and advice and large spirits, stretch us and help us to understand our bewildering selves.* This is no small gift; they deserve to be commended and recognized, too.

Chapter III

In-School Programs

AFTER giving you some idea about what goes on around and inside some of us, we now want to get down to the other half of our charge. That is, to come up with "a constructive response to concerns about the education of 'gifted and talented' children"—in other words, what happens in the classroom.

There are lots of ways in which gifted kids can help themselves, and we will try through personal recollection to point out some strategies and options available to you. We're convinced (against all logic) that what we've been through can help you organize your life a little better. Or help you to satisfy that insatiable curiosity and avoid the patches of grinding boredom that do crop up.

In the next two chapters, we give the pros and cons of some school experiences, plus some options we'd like to see. If you are like us, your school may offer all the options we mention and more (a lot of us have been lucky). Your school may offer some or maybe none at all, which was the case of one of our group, who *really had* to go outside the school system on his own to get some intellectual stimulation. (We think it is greatly to his credit that he didn't just give up or become bitter.) Our aim is to show you "gifties" that *you have decisions of your own to make, initiatives you can take, no matter what your situation is.*

As for our adult readers, particularly those in education, bear with us. We know that some of the material in this chapter is probably old stuff to you and that a few of the ideas we have dreamed up will come over as "impractical." But listen! We put them in here because we think you ought to know which programs do and don't work for us and why. Who else can tell you? As for our suggested programs, of course, we haven't developed great blueprints—that's not our job, it is yours. But maybe you can take some of our "impractical" notions and polish them so they *will* work. We feel strongly about them, so we believe we deserve a hearing.

First, let's start with the standard fare in any high school. If there are three to five million gifted kids in this country, it stands to reason that's all a lot of us get—standard fare.

Required Courses vs. Elective Courses

Fulfilling standard requirements for graduation in standard courses is just where a lot of gifted kids bog down. We can go through the motions easily enough, but often there just isn't enough there to stretch the imagination or to stimulate creativity. *If* we don't tune out altogether at this point, a lot of us knock off the requirements as fast as we can and then fill up on elective courses, *if* we can manage to squeeze enough time in to do so, and *if* there are a variety of interesting electives offered at our school. Three big "ifs."

Believe it or not, we don't necessarily want to reduce the number of required courses (at least some of us do not). They are part of the intellectual equipment of each and every citizen, whether bound for college or not. Of course, we want to delve deeply into our own interests and for those of us who tend to fix on one field to the exclusion of all others, required courses are an okay way to make sure we explore subject areas we have not been exposed to or would avoid if given the chance. But must we be held to the same timetable as others, e.g., so many hours or months or years of a certain subject if we are able to grasp the fundamentals and move on to a more complex treatment? Or to a new subject altogether?

We have already mentioned at least one instance in which one of us bargained for and obtained the option of receiving credit for a required course by passing the final exam. There have to be more places where gifted students can be accommodated in that fashion. For example, why can we not receive credit for private instruction when our schools are unable to provide the individual coaching we need, particularly in art, music,

69

or dance? A lot of us could pass proficiency tests in other required subjects that would free us to pursue new fields or advanced work.

We also wonder if one reason required courses are so often boring is that they bore our teachers too. How often is the dust shaken out and the routine changed? Is it that they are *the* basic elementary courses that they get cast in bronze and often receive less attention from the school board or faculty than the latest teaching tools? Who gets to teach the fun courses—not the rookies, in our experience. Why are not the best and brightest teachers in there mixing it up with the beginners (teachers *and* students) at least part of the time?

Electives are the best way—sometimes the only way—to expand on the restrictiveness of required courses in a regular school. By being allowed to choose their own courses, students gain independence and decision-making powers which are in and of themselves a learning experience. Free choice both enhances the gifted student's enjoyment of a course and increases his motivation. In addition, since many of us are pulled in all directions, wider exposure to many areas enables us to sharpen our personal goals.

We intend to discuss this subject in more detail in succeeding chapters. For now, we want to stress the need for more elective options and greater flexibility in the ways we fulfill required standards. It is up to us, of course, and to you "gifties" out there to explore right now how flexible your school is or can be. *If you don't ask, you're never going to know.*

In-School Programs

SPECIAL SCHOOL PROGRAMS

Special courses or programs for bright kids vary from community to community because of differences in the attitudes of staff, parents, students, and differences in available resources. The programs also range from minor changes in traditional patterns to broad departures from procedures established for the average student.

Though these programs and special opportunities are designed mainly to allow students (as opposed to "gifted") to extend their range, they are appropriate for us too—sort of.

One opportunity for alternative course work is through independent study programs; all too infrequently this includes tutorial work with someone outside the school. Another is through advanced placement (college level) courses given in high school. Also, a few of us have been admitted to courses at local colleges or universities while still in junior high or high school.

Moving a student along to more advanced work through alternative pacing usually amounts to skipping grades in elementary school and doubling up in high school on required courses so that they are eligible to graduate early. We have been there, too.

Then there are alternative schools—and you will have noticed that some of us are in special schools for the gifted or talented. Skipping can occur there, too.

The following pages present programs and the experience of various students in them. We cover in-

71

dependent study in a high school setting here, with the exception of our first example—which hardly fits in any place, it is so unusual. In a later chapter, we will describe some formal independent study experiences in the community, some under the direction of tutors or advisors other than our high school faculty.

Independent Study

In the fifth grade, I once engaged in a one-to-one tutorial experience which was very rewarding. The teacher was a really dynamic guy at the Maryland Academy of Sciences who taught me basic computer science techniques. At age 11, I would not have had nerve enough to initiate such a learning partnership (or know how), but I became acquainted with my tutor at the urging of a fantastic teacher who must have thought it was the right thing to do at the right time. It was sort of an *ad hoc* arrangement, but it worked.

A one-to-one learning experience is a really beautiful thing, because, for one thing, you cannot put each other on; there is a direct interaction of minds and there is no place for shoddy efforts on either part. There is especially no place for "mechanical" teaching or rote learning.

The benefits of a tutorial are innumerable; I have mentioned only a few here. If you have the chance and *if you have the motivation, make the chance!* Such an experience can be an incomparable one. I wish more elementary school teachers were alive to its merits.

━━━━

Mere interest or ambition is not nearly sufficient to allow one entrance to the elite independent study group at my school. One must have a certain IQ score (this, to me, is an ambiguous system), a certain grade point average (what of genius under-achievers?), and satisfactory teacher recommendations. That last one is a killer, too. I do not feel one's personality should be judged to win a few hours of time to learn if one craves them.

A better way, it seems to me, would be to have a panel of advisors who could interview interested students about their own independent program proposals and, after judging their ideas and capabilities, decide which ones could handle the independent situation. The other way around, you have to beat the standard system—which turns some kids into zombies—before you can exercise any initiative of your own. Sometimes that's all we need to make life (and learning) interesting in the required classes.

An independent study program is definitely an asset, since it allows freedom to work on what you want and at what speed you wish. For instance, I am currently monitoring the pollution levels of local streams and rivers. This is especially gratifying because the data actually does some good. This is *the* reward for often boring work. The results are given to the conservation commission of our town where they are reviewed and published. Something is accomplished; whether they know it or not, people are benefitting. Working for a high grade is not nearly as exciting as *seeing* your work help others. It's really a great personal lift.

━━━━

My Russian course this year is one of the most exciting courses I have ever taken because I am the only student in it. The course turned into an independent study experience by accident: all of my classmates graduated last year. I thought I would feel lonely in a class all by myself, but instead I discovered some fantastic advantages. First, I have complete control over what I want to study. Sometimes that can be a disadvantage when I try to do far more than I can handle because I am so excited by the material.

For example, right now, I am tackling four areas of concentration at once, as I have become fascinated by each one. They are: classical poetry (Pushkin, Lermontov, and old fables), modern short stories (which are nothing short of bizarre), a review of grammar, and general cultural studies, such as songs and newspaper articles.

Each week I am the one who decides what to work on. My teacher does not walk into the classroom and say, "Now we will study such and such . . ." Instead we have an informal class in one of the available offices. My teacher answers my questions from the reading, and we discuss what I have read from a literary point of view. Not only do I have complete control over what I study, but also I have complete responsibility—there's no way I can hide behind other students and not prepare my reading. By myself in a class like this I can go completely at my own pace and do just what I want to, which is enormously stimulating.

In tenth grade, I decided to meet my scientific interests by taking independent studies in physics and advanced biology. My primary interest was in an investigation of the effect of ultrasonic sound on plants. I was young and inexperienced and often quite lost—and my advisor was not much more sophisticated about the subject I had carved out. But I grew. The interdisciplinary world of science opened its doors to me and I learned where information could be found and how to get it. *Furthermore, I began to develop that fundamental quality of all successful studies, self-discipline.*

This year, as a senior, I am in an Independent Learning Experience program, one of many administered by the Hamden-New Haven Cooperative Education Center. Since all my work is away from my high school, I will describe that program and my experiences later.

My experience in independent study happened to be in physical education, a required course for most high school students and one which is often less than stimulating for average students, let alone the gifted. (I still feel self-conscious with that label.)

I have always considered myself an athletically inclined person. However, the sports I'm interested in—waterskiing, snowskiing, and sailing—are often not included in the curricular and extracurricular athletic programs. Consequently, I have little or no interest in high school sports, not to mention physical education classes themselves.

In search for an alternative way to get P.E. credit, I investigated the possibility of doing a contract course which would allow me to work in areas I'm interested in. For those of you who haven't come across this option, a contract course is just that: a student and teacher agree on the kind of work the student will perform and the length of time it will take; both sign the agreement or contract to that effect. Upon completion of the contract, "payment" is made in the form of a grade and course credit, according to how well the student has performed in living up to his part of the bargain.

To set up the contract, I went to my counselor to get the necessary forms and then proceeded to the athletic department. There I found the departmental chairman, sat down with him and planned my course.

I chose sailing for my unit since I had been involved with it for almost every summer of my life, and I knew I would be sailing during all the coming summers. Sailing is, however, something most non-sailors know little about, including the departmental chairman. Therefore, I had to set my objectives on my own.

I decided I would focus on sailing skills and techniques as demonstrated in the results of races throughout the forthcoming season. I would keep a log with entries for every race day to include: 1) general weather conditions (specifically wind speed and direction); 2) rigging according to the weather; 3) course position in relation to shoreline; 4) the side of the course or shoreline followed; and 5) the results of each race. Other features would include such things as regatta experiences and a general explanation of the Inland Lake Yachting Association, its rules and regulations, and the various classes of boats it includes.

After planning my objectives, we decided that all this would be compiled by the beginning of the next school year. I would submit a copy to the departmental chairman to be evaluated for credit. If I fulfilled my objectives, I would receive five to ten hours credit in P.E.

When summer came, I was a little reluctant to start immediately. After all, I had all that time. Why rush it! After two weeks of sitting on my duff, I finally decided (with a little pressure from my mother) to get going by recording general information on the type and size of inland boats I sail on and the organization of the Inland Lake Yachting Association. When the racing season started, I kept a little notebook on the various techniques used in every race. After compiling about ten pages of general information and eventually filling the notebook with technical skills appropriate to various situations, summer had come to an end.

It was then time to go back to school and have my contract evaluated. I was a little apprehensive about the athletic department chairman's reactions, but as someone with much interest in sailing but little knowledge, he was very impressed and gladly gave me my credit, thereby waiving the need for me to take a regular P.E. class ever again. And, not only did that notebook get me a grade and exemption from P.E., it has proved extremely helpful in rigging a boat when weather conditions are similar to those I observed and recorded.

*　—　—　*

Acceleration—To Skip or Not to Skip

In many parts of the country, it has long been traditional to advance gifted students in their studies by having them skip one or more grades—particularly those in the elementary school. Often this has been done without giving the student much warning, or providing much follow-up on his progress in the new grade. Such is seldom a problem in high school, since gifted students can and often do fulfill the normal requirements at a faster pace than their peers and are thus eligible to graduate early. Where more liberal graduation requirements prevail, they may simply forgo the senior year and proceed directly to college, where adjustment

78

problems are no longer the concern of high school counselors.

——

When I skipped a grade, I didn't do it in the usual fashion of returning to school in the fall one grade higher than usual. No, in my case some of the powers that be, namely my second grade teacher and the higher administration officials in the school, decided that I was going too fast. (You see, I was in Phonics Book F already instead of Book C—how exciting.) So in the middle of the year they decided that I was ready for third grade.

Intellectually, there was no problem and soon I even started doing extra work in subjects like math. Socially and emotionally, however, the change was a disaster. A major part of the problem was that I had been put into a class dominated by a ring of bullies, all socially more mature. And, if that wasn't bad enough, I felt even more insecure because this was my first year in New York City. This additional pressure, plus the mid-year timing (which would have been difficult for anyone) all added up to making me feel miserable. I didn't perk up for months.

Although skipping a grade was advantageous in meeting my intellectual needs and was probably a good move in the long run, I often wonder what effect that experience had on me socially and emotionally. With hindsight, it seems to me that those who decided I should skip should have considered more carefully my emotional readiness to do so. I also feel that by skipping I may have lost time in which I could have developed other skills, including writing.

- - - -

The very notion of skipping a grade is somewhat challenging, but unfortunately is also difficult to do.

When one is interested in skipping a grade (or two, or more), it is often very difficult to do without someone—a guidance counselor, a teacher, or any other person who has pull in your educational community—supporting the idea. It lends credence to your case to have good test scores, to "present yourself well" in interviews, and to have, again, a person who knows education behind you. Normally a principal's permission is the only requirement, but occasionally you must go higher, e.g., the local board of education. I don't personally see all this as good or bad, but face it, the "system" requires it, so you might as well be prepared if you or your parents want to pursue this course.

Having skipped five years in a variety of ways, I am currently (in May, 1975) age 15 and a sophomore at a major private university on the East Coast. I guess my first break came from the efforts of an extraordinary teacher whom I had in the fourth and fifth grades. The class itself, effectively homogeneously grouped, was one far above average in quality. For example, we collectively wrote, copyrighted, and saw printed a few dozen copies of a volume of creative writing. The situation was a wonderful elementary school atmosphere which dampened any social problems.

Unquestionably, a majority of the credit for my rapid progress must go to my teacher—truly gifted herself, consistently stimulating, and dauntless in her explorations on our behalf. I have described earlier how, through the efforts of this teacher, I was tutored in basic computer science. *

It was through my tutor, also a very gifted teacher, that I was introduced to the director of a special privately funded program for scientifically and mathematically gifted students. In due course, I became affiliated with that program. This man set up a now widely known fast-paced math class in which we covered three years of junior high math in one year.

After skipping seventh grade, I took an introductory computer science course at the local university in the spring of my eighth grade. Considering the drudgery that I had encountered in much of my junior high school work, this fascinating course was a truly stimulating experience.

Many of my eighth grade teachers reacted negatively when told of my plans to skip two more grades, all of whose fears have since been disproved. In the end, I spent one year in high school and then moved directly to the university.

In retrospect, my high school year was very en-

---

*Ed. note: As we go to press, this writer has completed his college work—in 2½ years.

joyable, socially. Despite being in an adequate intellectual environment, there was still a lack of serious study. *I did not really challenge myself to the extent that I do now in college; I did not really recognize a need for me to take charge, to a certain degree, of my own education and to make my own opportunities.*

To my mind, this may be the biggest advantage a good college has over a good high school. There, you *must* make your own decisions, you alone are responsible for seeking out those people and resources you need to educate yourself. For one thing, the resources are there; no high school can begin to touch them. Later on, I will elaborate on this point.

―――

By skipping, the student often feels alienated socially because he is younger than his classmates. *If socializing is of such great importance that adjustment is impossible, the advantages of acceleration are outweighed.* In this case, independent study, tutorial work, or some other form of advanced work should be considered.

On the other hand, many students find that they have no social problems, even after having skipped four and five years. Though I did not leave my peer group in high school, I have found myself in situations, usually playing in orchestras, where I have worked with people nearly twice my age. Most times, they respect my abilities and occasionally befriend me.

82

My school places students according to their abilities; accordingly, I have been accelerated in half of my subjects. Also, more advanced students are encouraged to take courses at the nearby city colleges.

I have felt less peer rejection in this high school than in earlier schools when age was the sole determinant for class assignments. (Peer rejection never bothered me, though; I've been a loner of my own volition.) My high school also specializes in the fine arts and music, so I am together with kids having similar interests.

I have been given the opportunity to skip four years but declined. My father, having skipped four times himself, persuaded me that I would find it impossible to date older girls. I'm not saying that I put more emphasis on socializing than education; in fact, I feel the reverse. But I did find alternatives so that I could have both.

***

Although I have never skipped a grade, I did have the option to graduate after the eleventh grade. I was counseled by the guidance office to go ahead and graduate early but I chose not to. I have quite a few reasons behind my decision. The main reason, although I hate to admit it, is that I was afraid. *In the regimentation of school, there is an odd security.* Skipping would be taking away your security blanket after it's been with you for eleven years. Which college? What are your future plans? What do you want in life? You've had to make no major decisions until now. All these questions bombard your brain, incessantly throbbing until you find answers. And those answers do not come easily. I felt I needed that last year to "get it all together."

There were some courses in my senior year which I was looking forward to taking. I feel the more I am exposed to, the better off I will be. There is always time for college, and behind the scenes, as usual, is the social aspect. I wanted to graduate with my class, with my friends. So—while most people are anxious to leave school, is there something wrong with me because I want to stay?

✦✦✦

A few months ago, I found out that I had almost completed my high school requirements and that I could graduate after my junior year. Though it may surprise people, I decided not to.

Why? I'm not mature enough. I can relate very well with people who are older than myself, but I have great difficulty with peer relationships. I feel intimidated by my peers, and tend to conceal any real feelings in order to be accepted by them. *I think I need another year to work out a balance between expressing my feelings and tactfully shutting up when necessary.*

It may seem that if I'm leaving high school, I don't need to be able to relate to high school students, but I feel there would be a gap in my life if I cannot come to better terms with myself and with what is, after all, a pretty large group of people.

So, although I could graduate early according to academic requirements, I have failed to complete my own personal and social development requirements. Everyone should consider this before early graduation. Some people may be ready for it, but others like myself may not be.

━╸━╸

Advanced Placement

The Advanced Placement (AP) program of the College Entrance Examination Board enables high school students to study certain subjects on a college level and to receive college credit for their work by passing an appropriate exam. While the program is not entirely for gifted students, many who participate are just that.

In her article "What College Students Say About Advanced Placement" (*The College Board Review*, No. 69, Fall, 1968 and No. 70, Winter 1968-69), Patricia Lund Casserly provides an evaluation of the program. Of the students from 252 secondary schools and 20 colleges interviewed by Ms. Casserly, about 90% reported that they had "raised their aspirations and increased their motivation as a result of their AP experience."

Seven or eight years later, our much smaller group would say the same. Why? Take one of the most popular courses, AP English, as an example: it offers richer material, more reading, more writing than the regular English course. And this is typical of all the courses. Moreover, AP courses are usually (although not always) taught by the best teacher. So if you want the best material and the best training, AP courses may be the place for you. We recommend them heartily.

Unfortunately, this option is not as widespread as it ought to be. The College Board says that about 3,783 high schools out of 21,763 offer Advanced Placement tests. And these figures are no real indication of the number of courses offered—a French boy taking an AP test in his native language can count for one high school of the total mentioned, when the high school had nothing to do with "advancing" his knowledge or fluency.

On the other hand, we know from our own experience and from the comments of students interviewed by Ms. Casserly that many students do take AP courses but *don't take the tests,* again skewing the figures above! This seems absurd, for omitting that last step negates some of the main purposes of the program—to provide some continuity between high school and college; to avoid repetition of course work already covered; and to allow for more flexibility in choosing college courses. In effect, advanced placement courses simply become honors courses, no more.

Students give various reasons for sidestepping advanced placement in this way. Some view the courses as good preparation for college generally. However, some of us see them as actual college courses, and not practice. Others take the AP courses because they are better than any others available, or because they are the next logical step in learning. Some students use AP courses as a kind of self-evaluation or exploration, or simply to have another piece of information to add to applications for college admission.

Not unusually, in the high school one of us attended which had an AP offering in nearly every subject, those few who did take the exams scored well above national norms.

Many of Ms. Casserly's students complained that their guidance counselors encouraged only top-ranking students and discouraged others from taking the AP tests so as to ensure high scores for the school. Though it has not been our experience, this seems to be another distortion of the purpose of the program.

Complaints or no, 90% of Ms. Casserly's sample still voted "yes" for advanced placement. On balance, we believe that AP is one of the best options around for an individual student to start exercising some control over his education. If AP courses are not offered at your school, start agitating. The program is well-established, so no one can call you a revolutionary. Find out if you are eligible to take any tests without the courses; maybe you already speak German well; if not, you certainly can learn. That won't turn your school upside down—and you may find yourself ahead of the game.

Most of all, if you are already in AP courses, *take the tests!* Whose time are you wasting? It is your choice;

make it and do not let yourself be dissuaded by anyone. *We gifteds complain a lot about not being challenged but if you are like some of us, you can let things slide and fail to challenge yourself.* So we're hoping you won't let that happen.

～／～／～／

Combining College and High School Course Work

I'm a member of that minority who knew all through high school where my main interest lay. I have always loved the biological sciences and if everything goes according to plan, my career will be in that area.

Having already taken every course in the sciences and related areas offered by my school by the eleventh grade, I was forced to search elsewhere for additional projects and learning experiences. The first step was to let my concern be known to the school. I told them I felt that it was their responsibility to allow me somehow to take more science courses. After expressing interest in attending a certain local college, I got a school recommendation, gathered my transcripts and visited the man in charge of adult night classes. As a result, I received a scholarship of $250 for a semester-long biology course. At its end, I will receive four college credits that can be transferred to the college of my choice. This gives me a jump on my college career and familiarizes me with campus life.

I have had another informal exposure to college-level work. A friend, now in college, has a deep interest in herpetology. While I do not share his love for snakes, I do have a concern for the conservation of wildlife. I joined him on a project regarding copperhead snakes. These are one of the very few poisonous snakes in my area and there is much public ignorance and fright. Many are needlessly killed and their numbers are dwindling. We capture these creatures, record various data and apply an identifying number. We then release them.

Accurate records are kept on where they are found and how they exist. The information from this project is being compiled for a book to be written by an expert currently working in New Mexico. By working with this friend, I have attended various meetings and lectures meant to educate the public, and have also learned a good deal about research methods and fieldwork. Being around those proficient in your field of interest helps one become involved, as well. It boosts one's confidence to contribute to important work—you feel important, too.

SUMMARY

In looking back over this chapter, we may seem to have strayed a bit from the concerns of our prime audience, those troubled "gifteds" who are blocked by lack of opportunities in their schools or who perhaps have not been "discovered" as some of us have been.

Our examples, admittedly, reflect more about how we judge the special opportunities we have had rather than what you can do if there are none. As such, they are probably more appropriately addressed to school people than to you.

Nevertheless, we hope that you will take heart in learning, if you do not know already, that such programs as independent study and advanced placement are perfectly valid goals for you to push toward in your school, for they are useful. There are interested adults who are willing and able to help you if you take the trouble to seek them out. Grade skipping won't kill you, either—we have survived and even thrived on it.

In the next chapter, also concerned with in-school programs, we will try to cover a subject that is seldom connected with gifted students, career education. It is in that area that those of you who have been pushed toward achieving high academic goals in traditional subjects—or not pushed at all—may find your other interests addressed.

Chapter IV

In-School Programs: Career Education

THERE has been a lot of discussion about whether or not this chapter even belonged in a book about gifted and talented students. True, much of what we say here is equally applicable to all students. But we decided that in the end the chapter certainly did fit in for three reasons.

First, we haven't talked much yet about the gifted and talented student who is so overcome by frustration and boredom that he or she simply tunes out and drops out. This has not happened to any one of our group, fortunately, but it does happen. *There are a lot of kids so turned off by sleazy academic programs designed for the very average student that they are willing to try anything—except school.* We think that good career education programs may provide a safety net for such people—a kind of last chance to keep them in the system, a way for them to find out about themselves and maybe a way for others to recognize, *finally*, their gifts.

Secondly, we *have* talked about our tendencies to waffle around, to be pulled by many interests, and about those adults whose interests we share and who have been helpful to us. It occurred to us that vocational courses are one way to put us in touch with different people in different areas—and to bring a little reality into our world. Broad exposure is necessary to insure a sound introduction to all fields. What we want to emphasize here is that such *exposure need not be in academic fields exclusively.* A variety of outside opportunities allow us to decide better what we will choose as a career and how to relate what happens in the school years to one's life choices. We are no different from "normal" children in that we do eat—and to feel worthy, we need to know we can do *something* well.

A further reason we have for talking about career education is that these programs are funded far more heavily now than are programs for gifted and talented. We want to show you, both students and educators, what opportunities there are for us in such activities. This section continues this discussion of career education generally and includes some suggestions almost any school could adopt and from which almost any student could benefit. This general discussion is followed by one specific illustration of career education courses offered in New Mexico, and the experience of one of us in an early experiment in the big business world.

CAREER OPTIONS—NOW

One of the main purposes of our public schools is to help prepare us for the future. Some students will go to college, others to vocational and technical schools, and still others directly to jobs for which they feel best suited. Unfortunately, a large percentage of graduates from both high school and college find themselves with a job that is totally uninteresting and unsatisfying, if they find one at all.

Some people blame this on unstable economic conditions. This may be true in those areas of work where jobs are scarce. However, other fields are begging for people; hence this argument is only partially true.

To some of us, the main problem lies in these individuals themselves and their previous education—plus some social pressure. They simply do not know where to turn because they are unaware of what career options are available to them and are apprehensive about choosing a career they do not understand. If you are a student and already have an idea of what you would like to do after graduation, you are in a small minority.

For example, a weekly newspaper editor recently said that the only worthwhile thing he learned in college was how to use rubber cement. Unfortunately, he found his true interest too late. If he had known at the time of his high school graduation (or before) what field he would have liked to enter, he could have picked a college or university better suited to these interests and could have taken journalism, graphic arts, and communication courses which would have been beneficial. There are a lot of students now—including the gifted —in his shoes.

One force which prevents students from enrolling in career education programs in high school is a social one. There seems to be a stigma attached to participating in career education as opposed to preparing for and going to college, as some 30 to 50 percent of all high school graduates do. We maybe are in an era in which a college education is overvalued, and consequently vocational education programs are not in vogue.

Many students, however, have careers in which they have *strong* interests, strong enough to preclude their going to college. Such students, despite their gifts, tend to be ignored or overridden by parental or social pressures. "Get a good education, son . . . " usually means "Get a liberal arts, or an *anything*, degree." There is, though, a lot to be said for doing things well, and vocational education programs can contribute to that just as well as standard higher education. They can also prepare one for moving on to advanced technical schools.

Let's challenge and end the social stigma attached to vocational education programs.

Reprise—Electives vs. Required Courses

Here junior and senior high schools can play a vital

94

role by exposing students to any number of fields through elective courses and allowing for in-depth study of individual interests. Some of the problems and solutions presented here may be applicable to you or your school.

There is no reason that any school should judge for you and everyone else that one subject will be twice as beneficial to you as another. Yet, many courses which last the same length of time may receive only half as much credit needed toward graduation as do others. For example, a senior in a southern city plans to be a carpenter. He also has a strong interest in art and likes to draw in his spare time. Therefore, art and general industrial arts courses would be beneficial for him. Unfortunately, for him, though, both are only one-half unit subjects and he must take one or the other, as only one elective which does not receive a full unit is allowed.

In contrast to these two subjects (two out of many), fundamental math, typing, home economics, advanced chemistry, and other subjects do carry a full unit of credit. None of these or the other subjects mentioned would benefit him more than the two previously mentioned. He already knows fundamental math; he doesn't own a typewriter and never plans to; he probably couldn't get into home economics if he wanted, as it is traditionally a course for girls (just as in many parts of the country, girls can't get into an industrial arts course should they wish to do so); and he barely passed chemistry and would dread the thought of advanced courses. Quite disgusted, he finally looks down the list and checks off "Latin, full unit" thinking that he can always move to Latin America and speak the language if the carpentry business ever gets poor.

Let us then, for starters, end discrimination toward some subjects.

━━━━

Mini-courses

If the schools are able to redirect their resources or are able to obtain additional funds, I feel there is a program of studies which would be one of the most beneficial ever available to students.

Beginning in *junior high school*, there should be a series of "mini-courses" or vocational courses offered to all, including the gifted. Some could last a full semester, others only a few weeks. They would be directly related to the future of the students and could help them plan or at least have ideas and goals about their career. The time for students to start thinking about this is not after college graduation, but during junior and senior high school.

The courses would not be extremely vocational or technical in nature. Most students at this age will not have decided on a career; therefore, the mini-courses would acquaint them with possible options.

At the junior high school level, these mini-courses need not be elaborate and, naturally, they would depend on the resources of a given area. I think there should be as many as is possible, though. Below are three examples of how such classes might be set up:

Law and law enforcement. Content: exploration of how the law and justice system is handled in the community. Student contacts: judges, lawyers, policemen, bailiffs, private investigators. Activities: tours of courts, police buildings, jails, etc.

Sales and marketing. Content: examination of what it's like in the retail business world. Student contacts: large chain store owners, small businessmen, salesmen, advertising agency or newspaper representatives, wholesalers. Activities: tours of various types of retail and wholesale outlets in the city, etc.

Communications. Content: exploration of how mass communication comes about with sidelights on its impact where possible. Student contacts: journalists, photographers, announcers, cameramen, sound engineers, typesetters (and their union representatives), directors, producers. Activities: tours of newspaper offices, telephone and telegraph offices, radio and television stations, etc.

Similar mini-courses could be developed for the field of transportation, agriculture and agribusiness, manufacturing, health and social services, sanitation and the environment, arts and crafts, education, science and engineering—the list could go on for the next hundred pages.

It may seem simple-minded and a reversal of my former position as well, but there could (and I think should) be a mini-course on college life. Believe it or not, in junior high, a lot of kids have only a vague idea about what happens in college or what resources a college has—and some might not even know or dare to hope that there their consuming interest could be fulfilled. Remember, some gifted kids are undiscovered even by themselves; a visit to the local college or university could be an eye-opener.

Work/Study Programs

During the high school years, a person does not have the time or opportunity to explore different jobs. It is difficult to take a full course load at school and to try to hold down a job at the same time. Further, during the summer everyone wants a job, so there is little job selection during this otherwise free time.

To solve this problem, a work/study program could be established that would enable a student to take classes in the morning and work in the afternoon. Students might even get their jobs through the school. Employers could contact the school and give information on job openings. Through forms indicating career interests, counselors could then work with a particular student to match his interests with available opportunities.

I realize this would take up some precious school time, but I feel it would be beneficial for students to begin to determine career choices and to gain work experience. I also think this would help counter the all too real boredom students often feel.

Speaking for myself, this past school year might have been difficult if it hadn't been for the job I had. Perhaps there is something behind the Puritan belief—idle body, idle mind.

▰▰▰

Mini-Internships

It would be beneficial to high school students to visit, observe, and spend some time with various professionals or craftsmen. Through this brief exposure—of a day or two—they could be stimulated to read and investigate further those of specific interest.

A prospective law student could spend a day in a law office, in court, or in a law library. A mathematician could explore such professions as actuary science, banking or accounting. Students interested in engineering but unable to decide whether it be electrical, chemical or mechanical could audit classes at a university in these various fields or interview a person who is currently working in those areas.

Students spending the daylight hours five days a week in school are unable to visit and actually observe the occupations which interest them because these are also hours of operation of such businesses. Professionals and students could share evenings and weekends away from their study and work.

99

A student changes his mind about what profession he would like to pursue many times during the high school years. Opportunities to observe many different professions apart from the junior high school mini-courses can help, particularly as students approach college or school-leaving age.

━━━

Career Enrichment Program

When I returned to Albuquerque after our first meeting, I found out that a new program was going to be started for the coming school year. This is called the Career Enrichment Program, which will be held at the Career Enrichment Center. The CEC is a district-wide center. It provides additional opportunities for highly motivated juniors and seniors with specialized needs and interests in an academic, vocation, or avocational area. The Center provides courses that a high school cannot offer because of the need for special facilities or where the demand in the high school is insufficient to justify the class. Transportation is provided to and from the Center.

A counseling and guidance program assists students in career planning for the present and the future, whether the student's goal is vocational or college preparation. A computerized data retrieval system will provide students with instantaneous access to information about occupations, college, and financial aid programs.

The Career Enrichment Center will also include the existing Dial-A-Teen program. Counselors from the New Mexico Employment Security Commission will also provide assistance to students for part-time and eventually full-time employment.

The following classes are offered at the Career Enrichment Center:

Advanced French
Latin
Italian
Beginning German
Advanced German
Navajo
Japanese
Advanced Spanish
Business Spanish
Communication in
    Spanish for
    Health Careers
Russian — Level I

Electronic Data
    Processing and
    Data Entry
Word Processing
Scientific Programming
Business Programming
Computer Tech Aides

Aerospace Education

Astrophysics
Physics I
Physics of the Electron,
    Atom and Nucleus

An Introduction to
    Qualitative and Quan-
    titative Chemistry
An Introduction to
    Organic and Bio-
    Chemistry

Multi-Science Careers
    a. Field Botany
    b. Genetics &
        Evolution
    c. Cytogenetics

Microbiology

101

Epidemiology
The Human Animal

Introduction to Geology
— Our Earth

Trigonometry
Analytic Geometry
Calculus
Probability and Statistics

Surveying I
Mathematics for
Surveying I

Environmental Survey
Cluster

Servicing Electrical
Appliances and Motors

Beauty Culture

Digital Electronics
Solid State Electronics
Communication Elec-
tronics

Each class is offered at four different times, and a student may attend any of the four sessions that suits his schedule. All classes offered count as three credits toward high school requirements.

We need something like the Center—and the Career Enrichment Program—in New Mexico because our state is sparsely populated, not too rich, and our high schools and communities alone could never provide us with this kind of service or resources. There is no reason, though, why other towns could not set up something similar.

Explorers Program

I was in a data processing post in the Explorers Program, a branch of the Boy Scouts. The post concerned itself with all aspects of data processing, with a definite career orientation. The corporation which sponsored our post provided both advisors and a huge amount of raw resource material to us. For reasons within the post (namely the striking personality conflicts of two members with the rest of the group), we folded after about a year, but the experience (and Explorers Program) lives on with impressive success.

The program is an excellent intellectual and social experience for the students involved. It provides an opportunity for students to explore *realistically* the career opportunities in the company's field, while enhancing the company's public image. Through a regional Explorers council, companies even search out, by various methods, students with particular interests.

I would highly recommend such a program.

I have always been interested in medicine and, through a career interest form I filled out in school, I was contacted by a local hospital to take part in a program sponsored by a local Explorers Post.

We had meetings once a week at the hospital, where we would hear a wide variety of medical specialists. During the rest of the week we would set up times when we would work in different areas of the hospital such as radiology, physical therapy, emergency room, etc. *This was a very good experience for me, since it allowed me to get a sort of a feel of different health and medical fields.*

This same program is now offered as a class at my school.

꧁꧂

I feel it is very important to get the student involved in extra activities that are related to school programs. This experience should be put on the student's record by means of credit hours. Experience like this could have fantastic after effects for the student, the school, and society.

It would be extremely useful if every student indicated their career choice and interests on a form at the beginning and end of each school year. This information would help the counselor in working with the student to determine classes to take in preparation for the career he has chosen, or if the student was undecided about a career, the counselor could propose ideas related to other interests he has indicated.

꧁꧂

A Business Venture

At 17 I learned the truth about many people. I

104

went into business for myself with a friend. We filed a charter with the state and began our brainchild. We began work on building a hotel in a predominantly black neighborhood.

As partners we selected a beautiful piece of property next to the university located in the area. We contacted the owners of the property; they were willing to sell but not to 17-year-old children! Of course, our terms were not the greatest, but what could we do?

My partner, in a stroke of brilliance, decided to form a board of directors for the company. We selected nine men in the business community, gathered them together and told them our plans. Much to our surprise they were enthusiastic. As a matter of fact, one of the board members lets us borrow office space.

The company then issued stock to the board and thus we gained some operating capital. We returned to the owners of the property, offered them a meager sum for a one-year option. After much deliberation, the owners consented and we were rolling.

Next we contacted hotel chains who were much impressed with our package. They even flew down to see us. As can well be imagined, each time people saw us they went into mild shock—we were too, too young.

As high school seniors we do not give the impression of financial geniuses. We are not, we just started the snowball.

At this time we are awaiting financing for our 1.5 million dollar project. We are very optimistic, in fact, quite certain of our success. We will have to discuss our plans with others much older than us, much different from us, but we have nothing to be afraid of. *The worst they can do is say we're crazy.*

More often, people will help if you **have** something worthwhile. The most important businessmen in the community will listen if you have a good idea.

If it's a thought worthy of discussion, tell somebody. Don't be afraid to tell even the most important people; they are only people like yourself. If I had been afraid, this project may have never even been started.

People are the most abundant resource. Learn this for yourself. Learn to get along with people without fear because they want you to succeed.

SUMMARY

Until such time as our needs and interests are recognized and accepted by all school systems, it will be necessary for us to make our own chances and opportunities. We can't do much better than our last example on how to learn about business. Go do it yourself—but if you are not feeling that energetic, do not ignore or disdain any career or vocational educational programs that may be around. Try them, if only for the people you will meet.

If you are tempted to drop out of school, please don't—you may miss something. A better way, we think, would be to do a little heavy thinking about what you would rather do instead, to find someone in that field or occupation—in or out of school—who would be able and willing to work with you and give you pointers on what you still need to learn. Check out those Explorers Programs. There may be one near you. Dead-end jobs can be even more boring than school; *If you find out what the next steps are, you can prepare for them.* Good luck!

Chapter V

Other Options

AS you may have gathered by now, we do not necessarily believe that a school, even a special school, is the best or the only place in which a gifted student can be educated. Minors though we may be, there are resources in the community that we can tap—on our own.

Some of us are lucky enough to live in cities where schools actively collaborate with other institutions and identify people who can help us. Others have dream programs they'd like to see that open some of these doors for us.

Here, to supplement the examples we have already mentioned in prior chapters, we describe alternative types of educational programs, beginning with an initial vignette about a special school that includes community resources and activities in a curriculum designed for special talents and interests.

One essay provides an example of a joint school and community course of independent study one of us would like to see; another talks about apprenticeships. We also pinpoint the riches to be found in various media collections and the advantages of learning experiences using a multi-media approach. Finally, our college student makes his case for the university as a learning environment in more detail, in case any of you need more encouragement to take the plunge early. We hope these descriptions and comments will spark some ideas among you all, both students and educators.

═══

High School of Music and Art, New York City

I attend a high school that specializes in the fine arts and music. The main advantages of being a student in such an institution is that we are able to pursue our major interest for two to four hours *each* day in school. (Mine is music—I am the bassoonist who keeps turning up in these pages.) In addition, many of us devote equal time at home in independent and assigned practicing.

My school offers special music and art curricula in addition to English, math, language, science, and social science courses. We also have numerous electives in each area. Some examples in the academy (that just means our academic subject areas): "Existential Literature" and "Film Criticism"; ecology and physics courses; fifth year French and calculus. In music, there is jazz improvisation, music history, Renaissance and Medieval music, composition, jazz band, chorus (required) and

110

choir (classical and gospel). In art, there is advanced design and layout, art history (required), ceramics, and oil painting, to name only a few.

The school sends students and student groups to perform in the community. Also many students have their art works displayed throughout the area. We also go to concerts, museums, and lectures that are pertinent to our course of study. Frequently professional musicians and artists come to speak with us.

One of the most enjoyable aspects of this school for talented kids is that the faculty is anxious to modify the curriculum and program to meet our needs. A difficulty arises, though when faculty positions are awarded to people who are neither talented themselves nor have much tolerance for those who are. Jealousy, resentment, denigration of students often result; we, too, have to run the gauntlet occasionally.

Even though we are intended to be a special school, at times there are just not enough *really* talented kids to populate the school. This causes another kind of problem. We are a public school, after all, and in New York these days it would be hard to justify limiting the student body to 100 when the plant and staff will accommodate 2,200. (That is my estimate of the number of extraordinarily talented kids in school now.) Consequently, our school includes students who range from brilliant to only slightly above average, forcing us back to the familiar syndrome of the average ones slowing down the more talented. Given some of the grim alternatives, one of them being *no* High School of Music and

111

Art in New York, I don't view this problem as serious. As I've mentioned before, we are grouped by ability. Students of lesser ability do benefit from the school program, which is good, and we all profit from sharing our common interests. I bring up these problems only to point out that they can and do exist even in situations that might appear to be the ultimate in special provisions for the gifted and talented.

✦—✦—✦

Independent Learning Experience (ILE)

This is one of many programs administered by the Hamden–New Haven (Connecticut) Cooperative Education Center. Before telling you about my own experience, let me describe it briefly.

ILE is open to highly motivated students from three high schools in the area. Such students are those who have already completed their graduation requirements or those whose opportunities have been limited by lack of school funds for special programs—the gifted and talented, for example.

A student works around a core interest. Community resources are exploited to the fullest to make interdisciplinary study available. Actual attendance on a regular basis in high school is required. Evaluations are based on an end-of-year presentation of his work in the core interest area to a group of the student's choice, all chosen from his school, community, or the college in which he has worked. Letter grades signify the group's evaluation, along with comments on his work.

The application procedures are thorough, though not complicated. A student asks for a preliminary interview to develop his proposal and then presents his refined proposal in written form. Students currently in the ILE program review the next year's candidates along with teachers, who evaluate proposals of new students. Before final approval, the student has one last interview and, after acceptance, is pretty much on his own.

This year as an ILE student, I have taken three independent studies—in English, multi-variable calculus, and analysis and topology.

In English, I gained a background impossible to obtain at my high school. The intensity of the course, British Literature from Spenser to Woolf, was far beyond anything I had experienced before. While I've cursed it at times, it has opened new worlds for me, and I honestly believe it is the most important course I've ever taken.

Abstract math is almost ideally suited for independent study. The format of the course is remarkably simple. About twice every three weeks, I met with my advisor, a fifth year graduate student at Yale, for an hour. We discuss problems I've done and questions I have. While we are not especially close, we do have a good deal of respect for each other.

Socially, the effect of taking all independent study

or university courses has been significant. I'm hardly in my high school or in contact with other high school students. While I miss the interaction with other students, I no longer have the stifling feeling that goes with being part of the mass.

To both my high school and myself, I am often an enigma. Throughout much of the year, I've been in an identity crisis. Despite my often being miserably unhappy and very lonely, ILE has been a positive experience. I have closed some gaping holes in my education and learned to get up at 8:00 a.m. and work for five hours without having someone on my ass.

Most importantly, I've learned that I'm a lot more human than I ever thought I was. Companionship and peer stimulation, those mundane necessities, are just that, necessities. It is comfortable to know, though, that I can do a job on my own when I want to or when I must.

▬▬▬

Education Center for the Arts (ECA)

This is another Connecticut program I think you ought to know about, though I cannot add any personal comments. It is the brainchild of the Arts Council of Greater New Haven, which administers and sponsors numerous other arts activities in our area. There may be more like it around the country; it may be worth some of your time to find out what is available in your town.

Other Options

Several school systems (I don't know how many) send students to the ECA for instruction. Classes are from 12:00 to 2:30 in the afternoon and students receive one or two credits (and a letter grade) for their work. The teachers, all professional artists, are employed part-time. I don't know how they are paid or by whom but assume it is by the Arts Council, though it may be by the Board of Education. The classes are held in an old synagogue.

There are four areas covered in the program. In the visual arts, classes are offered in drawing, painting, photography, and sculpture. Other subject areas are theatre, dance, and music. Students can take courses in more than one subject area, and the program offers "inter-arts" group experience.

Application procedures are quite simple. A student just prepares a written essay on "why I want to attend ECA," and either presents a portfolio of his work or takes an audition. To tell the truth, I don't know who the judges are—it would have to be one or more of the ECA teachers and the schools must have some screening process as well.

This approach seems to me to be an excellent way to give students special classes and put them in touch with professionals.

＿＝＝＝＝＝＝

School/Community Collaboration

While going outside the school for learning experience is certainly worthwhile, members of the community may also be brought into the school to work with students—someone to discuss society's workings and to relate the things learned in school to more practical situations or, when possible, to actually teach classes in their areas of specialization. Lack of money sometimes prohibits doing this to any substantial degree, but people can be found who are willing to donate their time.

The best way to find people who are qualified and who have the time to donate is to go through the local Chamber of Commerce, museums, art councils, and other community organizations whose members may be interested. Believe it or not, almost any business or profession is run by people who are interested in what goes on in schools. *Given the opportunity, there are people who are extremely excited about being able to explain to a select group of students how they got where they are and the interesting aspects of their business or profession.*

I had the opportunity to be in an economics class where a businessman (found through the Chamber of Commerce) taught along with the usual teacher. The man came to class every day for a quarter of the school year to explain the practical applications of economics in the business world, after our regular teacher described theoretical economics concepts. At the end of the course, we left with a greater understanding of economics as it related to the real world. It was one of the most enriching classroom situations I have ever encountered and I would jump at the opportunity to do it again.

▬▬▬

A Four-Day Week

There is only one school in the country that I know of, though I am sure there must be others, that has an actual four-day academic work week—the North Carolina School of the Arts. Wednesday of every week is set aside strictly for arts classes. If there are no classes on this day in their major field, performing or visual arts students use the time for study, reading, rehearsal, etc. I find this mid-week break useful not only in my art but in my academic studies as well. Teachers can be found occasionally on that day to help independent study participants or for general counseling.

▬▬▬

Trading Schools

I live in a city but would like to trade places with a student from a rural area or small town. Or, it would be interesting to trade places with a student from another school in my own city. I would live at his home and go to his classes and he would do the same. It would be like a small scale American Field Service program. There is merit in living in another country and attending schools there, and I believe this could be done within our own country, in states and cities.

117

Apprenticeships

Apprenticeships must once again become an important part of education, especially for gifted and talented students, because of their need for a more personal instruction.

A working definition of an apprentice is a person, usually a minor, who learns an art or trade by working under the supervision of a skilled master for a period of time. This idea worked well for thousands of years. Sons followed in their fathers' footsteps by learning their trades or by being "bound out" to other craftsmen. The parents of children who showed a special talent, especially in the arts, made arrangements with a master for the child to live and work with his mentor together until the master felt the young person was skilled enough to make his own way. This informal arrangement finally evolved into a fixed period of seven years. Most apprenticeships faded away with the further development of schools and the coming of the Industrial Revolution.

I want to emphasize the personal aspect of apprenticeships and its importance for gifted and talented students as opposed to classes outside school or special programs in a group situation. When one works as an apprentice, he finds himself involved in "the real thing—the life style, the ups and downs of the person he is learning and working under." Even if he decides that the line of work is not for him in the long run, he still has been exposed to the way in which the master goes about his work and what it takes to succeed in a particular field.

I speak from my own experience as an apprentice to a weaver, which came about (not for seven years, of course) through my involvement with the arts. As I began to work with her, learning the skills as I went, I found myself with an increasing interest in the craft and a great admiration and respect for many craftsmen and artists. Through this association, I have gained new ideas and insights that I have never gotten in the classroom.

I believe working as an apprentice to someone with similar interests is ideal; I was exposed to views that were directed to me and my concerns exclusively.

There are apprenticeship programs today for students who want to learn a trade such as bricklaying, carpentry, and plumbing. There must be a way of encouraging creative people in many other specialized fields to use apprenticeship as a means of learning.

━━━

An Interdisciplinary Course

I have a fantasy program of an interdisciplinary independent study for the highly motivated student who feels he is wasting his time in school. The student would decide upon a project on a subject of extreme interest not currently covered in school. The project would involve several subjects to satisfy all graduation course requirements, and the student would utilize facilities in the community, e.g., colleges, experts, museums, libraries, films.

Two examples (reflecting my own interests) might be:

A. *Russian Culture*
   English requirement—Russian literature
   Music requirement—Balalaika
   Art requirement—Iconography
   Social science requirement—
      Russian Revolution
   Language requirement—Russian

B. *Chinese Culture*
   Language—Mandarin
   Art—Pottery of the Ming Dynasty
   History and social science—
      Buddhism and Confucism;
      their influence on society
   Science—Physiology
   Electives—Acupuncture (in Chinatown);
      Chinese cooking

Under my program, additional math and science requirements would be fulfilled in school, providing some contact with the school and preventing social isolation.

Admittedly, this dream program belongs in a city, which is where I live, but I don't think one course is unreasonable or too hard for a school to work out, particularly in that setting.

━━━━

The Multi-Media Approach

We believe that a gifted student can go far by exploring all the resources of various media—in school or in independent study with or without the sanction of a school program. There are vast collections out there in a form that is peculiarly adaptable to our needs.

The different forms of media each have their own characteristics. The written word we read, the spoken word we hear, the visual word we see. Each presents a unique concentration of information per unit of time.

It may take hours to read about a molecular structure and fully understand its concepts. But if the written word were reinforced by the spoken word, a specialist in the field could explain the concept more easily in less time. Further, a still photograph could give a concept of the molecule in space. A moving picture of the molecule could possibly explain its function in only a few minutes. This time factor is very important to us gifted students.

Let us take another example. It may take hours to completely understand and see a battlefield during the Korean War through the written word. The student then turns to the spoken word in the form of recordings or through an instructor. Then still photographs could possibly be used to give details about the area involved.

Through the photographs the positions of armaments and related information are placed in exact locations. A motion picture could also be used giving the student more detail.

Each step taken cuts down on the time needed to learn certain information. The student benefits tremendously: he learns in a shorter time span and he does not misinterpret the messages as easily; he also gets more than just factual material. The student receives a tangible view of ideas not possible to relate through words. Film in particular can produce a sensitivity to different lifestyles and peoples, creating an awareness impossible to achieve through any other way short of actually traveling.

Students must be made aware of the number of resources available to them. They need access to all types of media whether it ranges from a 1962 issue of *Time* to an old Marx Brothers' movie.

Gifted students could use viewing videotapes on a much broader basis. At the present time, they are used fairly extensively at the college level. Only occasionally when a movie or documentary is taped are they used in educating high school students. I don't know if there would be any copyright problems but good TV programs are a great educational tool.

There are many programs now in progress which concentrate on the media as a resource quite apart from school offerings. Many business firms have hoards of information available to interested persons, especially students. Libraries have guides leading to these and many other sources of information. Museums can be a gold mine; many are becoming more active in their educational and community programs. College libraries, film and broadcasting programs, ought to be explored for the tidbits they can offer.

▰▬▰▬▰

As a sidelight on the multi-media approach, we'd like to bring up two separate but related points.

The first has to do with audio-visual equipment and materials and making them available on a 24-hour basis. Many schools do not permit their removal from the library or school building. We wish this ruling could be abolished or, at least made more flexible so that we can pursue our interests on our own time and at our own rate. The stuff is supposed to be there to help us learn—let us get on with it.

Our second point has to do with our need to exchange ideas with others of our own kind. For some of us, one of the most valuable aspects of this Symposium was the opportunity to get to do that.

One way we could continue sharing is by exchanging tapes—cassettes probably—or maybe even video tapes if we are in a place where we have access to such equipment.

And I'd even like to try my hand at producing some panel discussions among people I find informative.

The sharing, of course, presupposes some method of finding one another—and zeroing in on someone who would want to trade. Working out that little detail is beyond us!

To get back to reality, if your school is into audio-visual instruction, you can exploit that to the fullest, but if TV courses and the library collection are too simple, get going and ask that department for help in getting loans of material more to your taste. Or, as we keep saying, ask around on your own.

The University As a Resource

After some thought, I have concluded that the main value of the university to gifted kids is twofold: its role in helping the gifted student learn about that aspect of himself, and its role in education in general.

Admittedly, my experience is heavily weighted in support of this hypothesis. I was "discovered" by an elementary school teacher, but my most rewarding learning experiences have occurred through a professor at the university I now attend. I have been very much in contact with him from the beginning. Though my situation is unusual, I think my point is significant. The great advantage in knowing someone who really knows giftedness is that you can learn about your own giftedness in a real and practical sense and get to know that aspect of yourself very well.

Most large universities seem to have at least one professor who maintains enough of an interest in gifted education to make him an accessible person to, say, an

124

average gifted student going to said university. Those of you who shy away from leaving high school early may have overlooked this aspect of college life.

My second point is simply that a university in general can provide an academic atmosphere more conducive to learning for the gifted student because it is first and foremost a place of learning, more so than any other, to my mind. The people and the resources are there—not back in your high school.

Take courage, give it a try.

Chapter VI

Methods of Change -- and You

WE started out by saying that we believe you can take more responsibility for your education and development. We have talked throughout this book about changes we would like to see made or that you could make yourself. It is only fair, then, that we wrap up with a little more detailed discussion about change itself, and a few more specific pointers on the ways we think you can put into practice the suggestions we have proposed.

Also, in a book written by twenty people teeming with ideas, there is inevitably the valid point that someone really wants to get off his chest that doesn't quite fit the general structure we set up. So, we have included an essay or two of that kind here. One is a statement on priorities in public education, another on the validity of participation in student government.

We again try to speak from experience. We know

127

that as gifted students we are a minority and that our group is only a minuscule sample of even that minority. *We are not so naive as to think that our efforts or yours are likely to change the course of American education, or that our psychological problems will not be alleviated unless our whole society changes (that will be the millennium), not to mention our own individual communities or schools. But we do believe in ourselves, and each person who has indicated some strategy or another believes that involving yourself is worth the effort, whatever the outcome.*

Change Within the School

Occasionally, students will throw themselves at the mercy of the faculty when they feel they have been treated unjustly or when they desire something. You may have, and you know we recommend speaking up. There are many ways to achieve a change; however, not all modes and action work.

Rational, logical thinking is usually an important key to change. To have a chance of convincing superiors of the merits of your cause, preliminary steps must be taken:

1. Be rational; radical action only works in war zones.
2. Ask opinions; get support from student leaders.
3. Do your research; be prepared for any questions when you go before the faculty.

4. Keep calm before the faculty. Anger only closes the door to understanding.
5. Learn to compromise.
6. Learn to accept defeat graciously because many times it is only temporary.

Before these six steps can be taken you must learn to be solid—don't let someone control you like putty in the hands of a child.

If something in the system is wrong, you can try to change it, but do it right and get help if it's too big. Remember that people forget martyrs, so know what you're doing.

⎯⎯⎯

Change in a Rural Setting

Living in a rural area has many advantages and disadvantages as far as education is concerned. The advantages are that one can establish a personal relationship with faculty and students because of the size of the school involved. One can generate action with government officials and community leaders because of special "personal" relationships. Consequently, one can personally get involved with the school board and local government to change and aid educational programs.

The disadvantages are that it is difficult to administer gifted and talented programs because of the size of the schools and the budget, and community resources are small and sometimes inadequate.

However, in our area, the disadvantages are slowly fading with new programs just starting which provide a fantastic "spark" for our gifted and talented.

If stimulating classes and opportunities have to be made available to gifted and talented students in your area and you want to push for them, the big question is how do *you* go about doing it?

First of all, in order for people to respond to a situation they must know about it. Your everyday, run-of-the-mill townsperson probably doesn't know what "gifted and talented" is and he may not care. *What surprised us is that many educators do not know or care about the problem.* Shocking, but true!

The first step, then, is to start an *awareness program* with literature and information that can be published in local newspapers and mass media. In rural areas, local newspaper and local radio and TV stations are pretty accessible.

The next step is to actually take *action* in your community. If your school board cuts the budget, and in the process cuts out gifted and talented students, get involved.

Express your opinion to the board, write editors, and *ask for public support.*

School functions provide excellent opportunities for members of the community to know the gifted and talented, as well as to show positive results from tax dollars. A science fair, arts festival, dramatic presentation, art display, performances by student musicians or even an international meal are just a few of the many possibilities.

A local newspaper provides an easy access to a large portion of the community. Either through an editorial or through a letter to the editor, one is able to express personal views on programs and innovative ideas for the schools. Through some form of an article, you will be able to contact other people in your town who agree with your opinions or who are interested in improving education.

It is useful to get the support of local organizations such as the PTA, the League of Women Voters or other civic organizations. Such organizations have an easier access to information and often have more prestige and clout within the community than a group of students would have. They might be able to bring about some changes in the school system more quickly. Religious leaders in the community are also beneficial allies to have since they give a cause respectability in the eyes of many townspeople.

Funding for public education is the concern of local governments and school boards as well as the state. Therefore, attending school committee meetings with other students is an excellent means of presenting constructive ideas and commenting about the situation in the school system. It is important that any statements made in favor of talented children are backed with some evidence and with logical forethought, so that you can meet intelligently any arguments against the need for special educational opportunities for the gifted. Campaigning and voting for sympathetic school committee members, as well as other local officials who will work for quality education, is another important means of getting some results in the community. If you are not of voting age, you can certainly gather information and campaign amongst the voters you know.

People can get involved in so many ways! They can use political pressure, lobbying, and the media. They can work for apprenticeship programs, demonstration sessions, and workshops in their own organizations. You might speak to organizations and civic clubs, or hold a picnic, political rally, or any other kind pf program to stimulate interest.

The whole idea is that concern for this kind of opportunity has to start somewhere and I say that is with the individual. Enthusiasm spreads like wildfire! That means that one can get people involved by being involved. Students can approach the principal, teachers, and other students with their concerns. (Notice, I said approach. Please do this with caution, and make sure you let people know you are speaking on behalf of others as well as yourself, otherwise they can revert to hostile behavior.) I think support can be obtained if one believes in what he is doing.

So, believer, be optimistic and keep working. It may take a while, but the more people there are to support and work for excellence in education, the better the chance for some constructive action in your area —sometime, even if it is not in time for you.

Methods of Change—And You

Working for School Alternatives

You may have a sense by now of some of the educational alternatives that work for some gifted students. Admittedly, some things might take action by a state legislature or might take years—long after you've departed the scene. Getting excited about a high school of the arts can be counterproductive if there is no possible way you will ever attend this type of school. But other alternatives are not so complicated. I think school and community collaboration in education for the gifted is one such area.

The goal of my section is to give a *method* for establishing a goal, to show you how you can go about getting something going for *you*, now.

The following series of steps hopefully presents a reasonable structure for implementing some changes.

1. Decide and define in general terms what you want to accomplish and why. Keep it simple and *possible*.
2. Gather a group of people interested in solving the same problem. If you are an artist, look for some artists; if it is another field, find some others active in it. The more influential these people, the better. Not all have to be pros, some might just be activists.
3. Conduct an extensive survey of the resources and existing programming in your geographical area pertaining to your topic. Check school board annual reports; college catalogs; museum programs;

133

business involvement in community organizations with an educational slant.

4. Attempt to stimulate and then *measure* interest among the potential benefactors of your program.

5. Reset your goals in accordance with the results of 3 and 4 as much as is practicable. Get the professional help you need from your Item 2 group for the next steps.

6. Make formal plans which must include:
   a) budget
   b) necessary materials
   c) necessary personnel
   d) location
   e) sponsoring organization, if not school by type at least

7. Set up a plan of action which must include ways to:
   a) involve necessary people not yet tapped
   b) obtain necessary materials
   c) influence the people who must be influenced
   d) obtain funds
   e) obtain space

8. Set a timetable for your plan of action.

9. Go to work.

I guarantee that *something* will happen as a result. You may or may not wind up with the program you had in mind in the beginning. You may not get beyond Step 3 or Step 4. Even so, you will have learned a good deal about yourself, about what you really need and want. Nothing like putting it down in black and white or spelling out your goals to someone else to clarify them. And you will find out about the resources of your community, people and otherwise. I am confident that you will uncover some outlet for your interest and a way to grow and maybe even the very people to help you.

Student Government As a Proving Ground

A friend of mine who is fifteen and has skipped three grades was elected student government president in his high school. Even though his performance afterwards was not particularly good, in my view, his election can perhaps be used as an example of the social acceptability of acceleration and giftedness.

As manager of his campaign, and unofficial manager of my sister's successful campaign the subsequent year, I got to know student government from a behind-the-scenes perspective. For somewhat personal reasons and also maybe because I was never around very long in junior high or high school, I have not been elected to any student office beyond elementary school. Yet, throughout my school years, I have remained active in student government in this way and believe it is an extremely useful activity. So do those in our group who have been student leaders in their schools.

One is often struck by the irony in the way peoples' means differ in their attempts to achieve that Lockeian utopia, the common good. This applies strikingly to student government as well as to all politics. Concerning physics, Werner Heisenberg observed that revolution is almost often effected by "trying to change as little as possible." (In *Across the Frontiers*, if anyone cares.) So it often goes in other areas. Pure idealism tends to be tempered by time into long-range idealism; from one big jump to a series of incremental changes by which to change the system substantially. Perhaps the most useful function of student government is to prepare one for these later aspects of life, which is less likely to be governed by one radical revolutionary change than by a series of evolutionary shifts, which may in the end culminate in the realization of the radical goal.

I would say, further, that the merit of student government has two immediate and distinct aspects: dealing with other students and working with adults such as faculty, administrators, and others.

Perhaps the most difficult aspect for student leaders is maintaining that perspective and *respecting* an adult's view simultaneously. This, however, is the essence of student government.

Let me make some helpful hints in dealing with adults. One must conform to some extent; perhaps a nicer word is compromise. In preparing some factual memorandum or report, good quality is vital. A sincere and realistic ("mature") presentation is always important, whether orally or in writing. Know your ideas and speak them with confidence and respect, when you do it at all. Feel *responsible*. A student leader represents, in a physical way, many students; you *are* responsible to them.

I should add, I suppose, that if one does not know something of the proper manner in which to deal with adults, it cannot be learned totally through reading my advice here. *"Hands-on" experience is the ultimate teacher* though, and one should work on that principle. Student government activities can provide you with that.

With some gifted students, particularly those who are generally accepted and respected by teachers (as opposed to their advisors alone), discrepancy between student and adult becomes less acute. But, as the problem of dealing with adults becomes less and less, another develops. This is dealing with students, or more accurately, dealing with those students and adults for whom your giftedness may seem a barrier. But this is just a problem requiring good community relations and is, I believe, a simple question of your assuming your proper responsibility to those whom you lead or want to lead. In other words, if you are in student government, it is up to *you* to make yourself clear to others and to try to reach them. Once more, the experience is one that will serve you later—it is one of the facts of our lives and we may as well begin in school to cope with it.

Changing Priorities in Education

There needs to be more money for public school education and a change in the priorities of its distribution.

In the early 1970's, the Jackson, Mississippi school

system experimented with a most confusing and expensive system of "innovative" education. At one time, schools in the area of the city were set up so that a number of schools served grades 1 through 4; another served grades 5, 6, and 9; another 10; another 7, 8, 11, and 12; another 9; another 7 and 8; and another, 11 and 12!

This system was generally unacceptable to the public since parents with large families could end up with children in five or six different schools according to zone. Included in the plan was the total redesigning of an old, large junior high school into one giant fifth and sixth grade center. This project drained the public school system of money for a number of years. Ironically, next year this fifth and sixth grade center will once again be a regular elementary school.

One extracurricular activity that did not suffer during the period of budget cuts that followed upon the innovation was athletics. The school system and booster clubs continued and still continue to pour in money to the various athletic teams.

Other areas of study were not so lucky, however. The art program at a local high school suffered greatly this year. Nine classes and two teachers had to split only $240 for art supplies. This, as well as the activity fund into which art students had to pay, was gone months before school was out. Students in many cases had to buy their own art materials. According to a local art teacher, the $240 figure compares with only $1,000 for five classes in 1970—still not a huge sum and certainly one not to be trimmed.

138

Other areas have it even harder. At my own high school, the school newspaper is not subsidized at all and must compete with about twenty other high school papers in the area for advertising. The school yearbook is not allowed to sell advertising at all, due to pressure put on the school system by business people. The literary magazine had to raise money on their own to publish their journal, the first issue in three years. The band has had to miss a number of out-of-town football games in the past few years; they are not included in the athletic fund-raising plan or their budget. Members of one club even sold themselves as "slaves" for two days to raise money for an educational trip.

The football team, of course, still continues to travel all over the state and eat at the finest restaurants free of charge.

Unfortunately, people who could afford to put more money into the schools won't vote for it because they patronize private and parochial schools.

If a similar situation exists in your area and money is short, let's at least try to get a reapportionment. You can start by drawing attention to the imbalances.

SUMMARY

We've said all we've got to say about our experiences, the changes we would like to see in our education, and how you can, as a gifted person, begin to help yourself. Now it's time to turn it over to you, our readers—and our critics. But not without a few parting words of our own.

In my opinion, we guys, twenty rarely coherent but highly sincere writers/editors, are the main point, if not the entire reason for being, of this book. This was not written by a learned professor, a committee of scholars assigned to the task by the best minds in American education, or by the wonderful people who brought you "Essentials of Algebra".

We wrote it. And we *lived* it. *That's* important.

Not any of the greatest minds in the field can claim to be a high school junior or senior and to be right now and on a day-to-day basis fighting with the problems and rewards of being "gifted and talented" in today's society.

We are. And we're still living it, concerned with salvaging the best education possible inside a system oriented toward the other 97%. Though we are only twenty, just consider that "*we*" as coming from the remaining 3% or 3 million gifted kids we feel we represent and you will know why I push the point.

A final word to our gifted readers—and we hope we find you. As we've said, we know it's not all shredded wheat—you can have hostile teachers, you can alienate yourself from peers. You can tell bratty kids that you're going to be a writer and they can cry "Oh, like John-Boy Walton!" and you can go to jail for justifiable homicide.

But the whole point of this book—more im-

140

portantly, the whole point of "gifted and talented"—is its limitless potential for good things. Literally, I feel like a peaceful use for the A-bomb every so often.

"Gifted and talented" is not something you can take up lightly on free weekends. It's something that's going to affect everything about your life, twenty-four hours a day, 365¼ days a year. It's something that can force you into being mature before you might be ready; it's something that can go all wrong on you and leave you torn apart.

But there are peaceful uses for atomic energy. There are good deeds to be done. There *are* opportunities waiting for you. "Gifted and talented" can be, basically, what you make it. But you can't just *sit* there. If you're willing to accept the responsibility, which is the prerequisite course around here, you can take off from there and really have a great time. Why not now?

━━━

141

Appendix A

RUDY AGUILAR
  Catholic High School
  Baton Rouge, Louisiana

LEAH ANN BARRON
  Breauxbridge Senior High School
  Breauxbridge, Louisiana

JIM BERGLUND
  East High School
  Lincoln, Nebraska

COLIN CAMERER
  Study of Mathematically and Scientifically
    Precocious Youth
  The Johns Hopkins University
  Baltimore, Maryland

Eric Cornwald
  St. Anne's Episcopal School
  Brooklyn, New York

Cynthia Grandison
  Walbrook Senior High School
  Baltimore, Maryland

Eric Grevstad
  Connard High School
  West Hartford, Connecticut

Ed Inman
  Murrah High School
  Jackson, Mississippi

Julie Kaufman
  Sharon High School
  Sharon, Massachusetts

Kenneth Lieberson
  High School of Music and Art
  New York, New York

Judith Matloff
  Hunter College Campus Schools
  New York, New York

Cherie Lee Onkst
  Dunedin Senior High School
  Dunedin, Florida

Denise Pinkston
  East High School
  Lincoln, Nebraska

List Of Authors

JOAN RISCHLING
  Southeast High School
  Lincoln, Nebraska

CAROL STEFANIK
  Canton Regional High School
  Collinsville, Connecticut

DIANE SYRETT
  North Carolina School of the Fine Arts
  Winston-Salem, North Carolina

DOMINIC TRUJILLO
  All Indian Pueblo Council
  Albuquerque, New Mexico

RAMONA WANYA
  All Indian Pueblo Council
  Albuquerque, New Mexico

HENRY WEBBER
  Lee High School
  New Haven, Connecticut

ELIZABETH WOOD
  St. Anne's Episcopal School
  Brooklyn, New York

Appendix B

CONSULTANTS*
NATIONAL STUDENT SYMPOSIUM ON THE
EDUCATION OF THE
GIFTED AND TALENTED

MARJORIE L. CRAIG
  Secretary
  The American Association for Gifted Children
  New York, New York

DR. DAVID M. JACKSON
  Executive Director
  National/State Leadership Training Institute on
    the Gifted and Talented
  Reston, Virginia

FELICE KAUFMAN
  Project Sparkle
  Norwich Public School System
  Norwich, Connecticut

*With positions held at the time of the Symposium

147

Everett Kinstler
Vice President
The National Arts Club
New York, New York

Mark L. Krueger
Office for Gifted and Talented
U. S. Office of Education
Washington, D.C.

Scott McVay
Executive Director
Robert Sterling Clark Foundation
New York, New York

Elizabeth Neuman
The American Association for Gifted Children
New York, New York

Naomi Noyes
Children's Specialist
Manhattan Branch Office
New York Public Library
New York, New York

Dr. Sidney J. Parnes
Professor of Creative Studies
State University College at Buffalo
Buffalo, New York

Margery W. Thompson
Editor
Washington, D.C.

Consultants and Panel Participants

JANE L. WARD
    Cambridge Communications Group, Inc.
    Cambridge, Massachusetts

JANE CASE WILLIAMS
    Deputy Director
    Office for Gifted and Talented
    U. S. Office of Education
    Washington, D.C.

PANEL PARTICIPANTS

THE HONORABLE JACK FAXON
    State Senator, 7th District
        and President Pro-Tempore
    The Senate of the State of Michigan
    Lansing, Michigan

AMAZIAH (BILL) HOWELL
    Staff Assistant
    The Office of the Honorable Senator James Buckley
    New York, New York

DR. CARL SAGAN
    Director
    Laboratory of Planetary Studies
    Cornell University
    Ithaca, New York

MURRY SIDLIN
    Resident Conductor
    The National Symphony Orchestra
    John F. Kennedy Center for the Performing Arts
    Washington, D.C.

ANNE E. IMPELLIZZERI, Chairman
  Health Education Consultant
  Metropolitan Life Insurance Company
  New York, New York

    Member of the Board
    The American Association for Gifted Children
    New York, New York